CAN THESE BONES LIVE

EDWARD DAHLBERG

With Forty-two Drawings by James Kearns
and a Preface by Sir Herbert Read

Ann Arbor Paperbacks
The University of Michigan Press

CAN THESE BONES LIVE

First edition as an Ann Arbor Paperback 1967
Copyright 1941, © 1960 by Edward Dahlberg
All rights reserved
Published in the United States of America by
The University of Michigan Press and simultaneously
in Rexdale, Canada, by Ambassador Books Limited
Manufactured in the United States of America

To the memory of
my Mother, Elizabeth Dahlberg, who,
as sorrowing Hagar, taught me
how to make Ishmael's Covenant with the Heart's Afflictions.

CONTENTS

LIST OF ILLUSTRATIONS   ix

PREFACE BY HERBERT READ   xi

I.   THE MAN-EATING FABLE   1

II. THOREAU AND WALDEN   9

III. RANDOLPH BOURNE: IN THE SADDLE
     OF ROSINANTE   27

IV. CAN THESE BONES LIVE   41

        1. Ishmael   43
        2. Sanctified Lies   51
        3. The Flesh Refused   55
        4. Zossima's Corpse   65
        5. The Helmet of Mambrino   69
        6. The Proletarian Eucharist   72
        7. Melanchtha   75
        8. Ezekiel's Valley   78

V.   THE BRIDEGROOM'S ACHE   89

        1. The Sink of Bethesda   91
        2. The False Ascension   93
        3. The Bridegroom   96

VI. THE CROSS AND THE WINDMILLS   107

VII. WOMAN   119

    1. "I was naked; and I hid"   121
    2. "The venom thou hast poured on me
        Be still, my spirit."   134
    3. "Sing O Barren"   142
    4. "False Cressid! false, false, false!"   150

VIII. SUPERSTITION AND IMAGES   165

    1. The Witch's Cauldron   167
    2. Statute Answer and Man Question   169
    3. The State Kettle   173

ILLUSTRATIONS

Edward Dahlberg   *facing title page*
Ixion   2
Hamlet   5
The Fool Who Is Truth   8
Thoreau   12
Sacco, Vanzetti and John Brown   14
"The mass of men lead lives of quiet desperation"   22
Randolph Bourne   28
Plato, Martin Luther, Marx, Lenin   36
Ishmael   42
Odysseus and His Mother   47
Poe   49
Moby Dick   54
There Is Only Man   57
Emily Dickinson   59
Henry Adams   64
Zossima's Corpse   65
The Helmet of Mambrino   72
The Kidneys, The Prostate Glands and the Intestinal
     Tract   77
Melville   81
Neon Lights   85
Christ   90

Christ	99
Judas Kissing Christ	103
Moses	105
Don Quixote, Sancho Panza and Christ	108
Sancho Panza Whipping Hedges	115
Hester	120
Ahab	123
Ahab	126
Billy Budd	131
Black Cat	138
Raven	141
Bee	142
Walt Whitman	147
Which Way Revolves the Wheel of Fire	151
Woman	154
Dostoevsky	158
Hitler	162
Romulus and Remus	166
Stalin	175
Sisyphean Rock	178

PREFACE by Sir Herbert Read

"*Walden,*" Mr. Dahlberg writes on one of the pages which
follow, "cannot be rushed into men's hearts . . . *persuade and
hint.*" I wish I could follow that advice in introducing this
edition of his own book. It is a book I have lived with now for
five years, and there is no contemporary prose work from
which I have got so much pleasure and profit. The pleasure
comes from the texture—a prose style which, in an age that has
forsaken the art of prose, gleams with rich expressive beauty.
There is not a page which lacks its vivid imagery, its memor-
able phrase. It is not the slick prose of the smart journalist,
nor the careful prose of the timid intellectual, and least of all
the intricate jewelry of the aesthete. It is the crystalline vein
of the English Bible, of Shakespeare and Sir Thomas Browne,
running through the torpid substance of modern life. It is not
writing for writing's sake: it circles round the pit of our misery
and degradation, and is as relevant to our present condition
as any book of wisdom, and far more relevant than the scientific analyses and political prescriptions which are the ration-
alizations we make of our moral bankruptcy.

It is this all-pervasive human wisdom which draws one to
the book again and again. It is a work of criticism and exposi-
tion. Shakespeare, Dostoevski, Cervantes, Thoreau, Melville,
Whitman, Rilke, Randolph Bourne (of whom we are so re-
grettably ignorant in England)—these are the prophets to be
expounded, related, excoriated (stripped of accretions of plati-
tude and misunderstanding). But behind them are the original
prophets, the great Hebrew prophets, and the greatest prophet
of them all, the Galilean. Turning and returning to these Hebraic forebears, Dahlberg taps some source of collective en-

ergy, some fire-laden force of anger and denunciation, some heaven-lit clarity of vision.

Some of us remember another book written by Edward Dahlberg, published nearly twenty years ago. It was called *Bottom Dogs,* and it had a long introduction by D. H. Lawrence. That book, as Lawrence said, was a *ne plus ultra,* and Céline's book, which came later and was more talked of, did not equal it in what Lawrence called "repulsive consciousness, consciousness in a state of repulsion." By comparison, *Can These Bones Live* is a charitable, though not a self-deceiving book. In the interval Dahlberg has drunk deep of the wisdom of the wisest European, Cervantes. But not Don Quixote, but Sancho Panza, is his hero. "The critic is the Sancho Panza to his master, our Lord Don Quixote, the artist. For only the Quixotist can be a true Sancho Panza. Sancho is no bread, butter and beer realist. He, too, sees with undersided sights and knows with the magical folly of the heart that there is knowledge before reason and science, a secret wisdom that is prior to logic—the vibrant god-telling PULSE." And then follows a paragraph which I have already quoted in one of my own books, and which seems to be the essence of my faith, of Dahlberg's faith, of the faith of anyone still anxious to avoid the snares of rationalization and superstition:

> *There are no abstract truths—no Mass Man, no proletariat. There is only Man. When the Pulse has been nailed upon the crossbeams, lo, Reason gives up its viable breath and becomes a wandering ghostly Error. Truth and folly are ever about to expire, so that we, like our beloved Sancho Panza, kneeling at the deathbed of Don Quixote, must always be ready to go out to receive the holy communion of cudgels and distaffs, for the rebirth of the Pulse.*

THE MAN-EATING FABLE

"The canker-blooms have full as deep a dye
As the perfumed tincture of the roses."

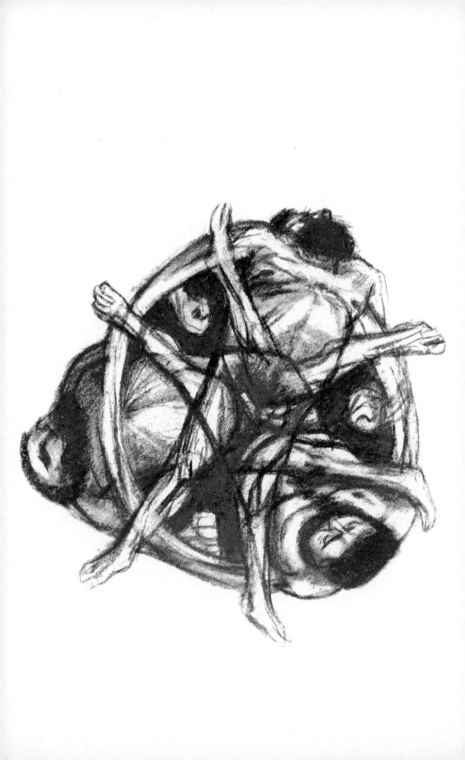

Truth, Good and Evil revolve like the perpetual wheel to which Ixion was bound. Tamburlaine, the "Scythian thief," sprinkles Asiatic lands with the brains of men, and thirsts for the far infinities of the Milky Way; unambitious and loving Hamlet, who can "be bounded in a nutshell, and count myself a king of infinite space," embitters the earth; Macbeth speaks truths from Gothic caves of terror; the evil and saturnine Ahab, soaked in a metaphysical revenge and in blood "older than the Pharaohs'," knows moral ecstasies as tender as ". . . let me look into a human eye; it is better than to gaze into the sea and sky; better than to gaze upon God." Resolve these ambiguities who can?

We look at *Timon of Athens* and *Hamlet* for the light and the darkness. That man-eating tragedy, *Timon of Athens*, is not a play, but a Last Supper of Hate; and *Hamlet* is Shakespeare's own Gethsemane. Hate befouls Timon and deprives the world of a most fragrant nature; generous, warm-livered Timon, who banishes himself from Athens because the lords devoured his silver and substance, feeds his malice and so starves himself to death. Hamlet is prey to a revenging ghost that sups on his mercies and wastes Hamlet's heart in its own consuming malignity. The iniquity of Hamlet is not in Hamlet, but in his father's ghost. Death's logic is implacable; ghosts are more remorseless than men and do not return to the world with the olive branch and the honey of the Elysian meadows in their night-substanced souls. When Odysseus visited the underworld he "dug a trench and poured into it the blood of the black victims," for the shades have neither speech nor memories until they have drunk man's blood. Macbeth racked by Banquo's Ghost moans:

> If charnel-houses and our graves must send
> Those that we bury back, our monuments
> Shall be the maws of kites.

Hamlet is loving, and it is a sinful irony that men have called Hamlet weak and pithless—meshed in star-foamed ambiguities and melancholy—because he hesitates to kill. The hells of the world broil Hamlet's blood into red-hot tears and into an insanity of remorseless pity; let him who has tasted the sulphurous broth of his grief say that Hamlet's malady belongs to a green unripe brain.

The Dumb Show is Hamlet's Conscience, but it is also the Ghost's bodkin. It is the ruse of a baited spirit; it is the cage in which the King's Guilt and Hamlet's Will are both proved. This is the PLAY: if Hamlet can catch the King's conscience in the purgative DUMB SHOW, in the MOUSE TRAP, if he can dissever the reechy and incestuous union between his mother and his uncle and starve the owner of the crime of his gains, he has made Guilt shed its shame and has disburdened his own heart.

To satiate the Ghost, Hamlet has no other course except to spill blood and exchange a lover's moral rage for endless nausea. The most drab and pathetic letting of blood is the murder of Polonius behind the arras. Hamlet's bowels are sick—the seeming-calloused Hamlet trumpets: "I'll lug the guts into the neighbour room."

Hamlet has all the will to tell the truth and less than

none to assassinate. There is no wavering Hamletism in
Hamlet; he ensnares his uncle and plays upon the players,
Guildenstern, Polonius and Ophelia, who play upon him.
Ophelia's feigning is as futile as Guildenstern's politics or
as Polonius's arras-minded statesmanship.

Nor does Hamlet wait, once he knows, to hold the
mirror up to his mother's concupiscent nature. Hamlet
runs into her room, the contagion of her lewdness feeding
his wrath—the bone and flesh pity of the son overpowers
all else—and pours forth: "Mother, mother, mother!" Little
in the literature of sorrow, save in Ibsen's *Ghosts*, in those

grief-stabbing and eternally spun-out pities, "Give me the sun, the sun, the sun!" so wrings the humanities from us.

Hamlet is sick; his tragedy is that, unlike Alyosha Karamazov's, he does not know the physic for all the soul-diseased culprits of the world: "Do you know, Lise, my elder told me once to care for most people exactly as one would for children, and for some of them as one would for the sick in hospitals."

Hamlet's sorrow is our horoscope, so much we know; but history does not improve man and auguries do not make him wiser. Saul and Macbeth become darksome figures when the Fates unravel their purposes. Hamlet forswears his nature, the moon, the stars and Ophelia, for the Stygian revenge of a Ghost. The death of Polonius, the lunacy of Ophelia, so soon to drown and lie in sweeping water among her flower kin, long purples and daisies, knit together Hamlet's infernal destiny. The PLOT infolds each figure in its DEMON CLAWS and all, the King, the Queen, Laertes and Hamlet, succumb.

Hamlet, Macbeth and Timon—these are our fables, the proverbs, the Golgothas we have memorized; but history, the ACT, is the sign of Cain. Terror is the lodestone, and its mark is in the first blood-besmeared pictures in the Paleolithic caves, in human sacrifice, in murder and war. Shakespeare and Goya forced men to cringe before their own dark beast abysses. We cower as we look at Goya's *Saturn Devouring His Son* or at his painting of the officer regarding with carnivorous satisfaction the simple soldier hanging from a tree—as we hear Timon's ultimate blasphemy: "Nor on the beasts themselves, the birds and fishes; you must eat men." These are the tragical MOUSE-TRAP paintings and plays to bait the conscience of men.

There is a direful myth that Shakespeare lost his reason

and disappeared before he died. The legend is in the text if not in the life. The Shades and the Weird Sisters supped upon that globular and vasty brain until it was emptied of its reason and expired in the sound and fury of the "tale." Shakespeare was the "Heartbreak Poet" to Keats; he was as crucified as Hamlet, and as vulnerable as Lear. He died not from venom but, like Lear, expired when the Fool, who is Truth, was hanged, and Cordelia, who is Faith, was slain. Shakespeare did not write the PLAYS; life wrote them, and then drove him mad.

Man is in constant mourning over corpse ideals. In this mood he mantles his heart in an iron shroud of negations and yields assent to the hypochondriacal declamation of Sir Thomas Browne: "But man is a Noble Animal, splendid in ashes, pompous in his grave." But no matter how disenchanted man becomes, he does not forswear the legendary course of the heart. He cannot. Man pursues a desperado philosophy of gallant idealism, and lives and hopes and cankers with a defiant flourish. With inextinguishable fervor he ceaselessly creates his cycles of sonnets, music, art, ethics, and then with a chivalric irony wraps the WORMS in the GOLDEN FLEECE OF COLCHIS. This is his eternal battle of valiant desperation against all palpable and unknown limits.

Some men, like Machiavelli, impose armored limits upon themselves; and, though they imprison their spirits in redoubtable theorems and logic, their lives contradict their sternest realities. These irreconcilables exist in the seemingly axiomatic *Prince*, that compound of Borgian horror spectacle and dragon-toothed maxims, which advise the prince and so betray him. Machiavelli himself was a fanged demon with tender, milk-white morals; and his

GOTHIC SHOCKERS, those pen and poison portraits, are as baffling as the beast and man tragedy in the world.

Good and evil are inseparable; beast and man are sewn together with threads of heaven. The fable of the Centaur Chiron, who nursed Achilles, becomes the awful parable in *Timon of Athens*. Shakespeare took almost line for line the lion and the fox precepts in *The Prince:*—Timon says, "If thou wert the lion, the fox would beguile thee; if thou wert the lamb, the fox would eat thee." But in *Timon* the anthropophagous acts of man become the terrible Sermon on the Mount of hate. Timon cannot hate without eating himself and thus making his own tomb.

II

THOREAU AND WALDEN

We cannot perceive what we canonize. The citizen secures himself against genius by icon worship. By the touch of Circe's wand, the divine troublemakers are translated into porcine stone embroidery. Think how Thoreau and *Walden* have been shunned. *Walden,* the purest parable ever written in America, remains shut. However, *Walden,* which takes its inspiration from the Vedas, is the secular bible of our ethics. What it hints of—*how* to resist evil, society, patriotism, poverty and war—we dare no more neglect. How to resist? Therein lie all the morals and all the terror of this world.

There is an uncanny shrewdness in those well-governmented Americans who have looked at Thoreau as a kind of cranky male sybil, a crabbed and catarrhal water sprite of our woodland culture. Little wonder that his "Civil Disobedience" lies dormant and half forgotten as a curio in libertarian and anarchist anthologies. Imagine were it otherwise: what state would dare render sincere homage to its greatest malefactor, Henry David Thoreau? What society of men so beautifully groomed in submission could countenance "Civil Disobedience": "How does it become a man to behave toward this American government today? I answer, that he cannot without disgust be associated with it. I cannot for an instant recognize that political organization as my government which is the *slave's* government also."

How unconsciously astute is the Massachusetts Commonwealth to garment Thoreau, an anarchist and militant defender of Captain John Brown, in marble robes while mortally detesting John Brown, and in our own lifetime executing those simple pure apostles of free men, the shoemaker and the fish peddler, Sacco and Vanzetti. His Journals overflow with such anathemas as: "My thoughts are murder to the State; I endeavor in vain to observe nature; my thoughts involuntarily go plotting against the State. I trust that all just men will conspire." And his curses fillip the stars whenever the dust of his native place is upon his tongue: "As for Massachusetts, that huge she-Briareus, Argus and Colchian Dragon conjoined, set to watch the Heifer of the Constitution and the Golden Fleece, we would not warrant our respect for her, like

some compositions to preserve its qualities through all weathers."

The State is adept in the mysteries of evasion and interment. Henry David Thoreau is honored; but his books lie buried like the fresh barley seeds stored by Joseph in granaries and scattered in Pharaohs' tombs. Administrative Philistia needs no economic astrologer to help it read "Civil Disobedience" or *Walden*. Society is clairvoyant, knows how to govern, when to load its musket, when to erect an obelisk—and when to canonize. The antiquarian is the State's best servant and art's most formidable foe. Sequester the writer, make him an "early American" of a Golden Age of Letters, and you refuse him. You disclaim him by a spurious exaltation of his period.

Writes Hans Ryner: "We say that the age of Pericles was magnificent. Yet Pericles was the object of all sorts of accusations. Phidias was prosecuted; Anaxagoras was exiled; Socrates drank the hemlock." The artist in any age is a divine accident. In what time and place was Herman Melville's genius born: whence came this Job? this creator of the Cabala of Whaling Science? Where is the American signature furrowed in Henry Thoreau's Himalayan brow? "The social condition of genius," wrote Thoreau, "is the same in all ages. Aeschylus was undoubtedly alone and without sympathy in his simple reverence for the mystery of the universe." No other American but Bourne has taken such a deep and accurate measure of the secular despotisms of government as Thoreau. None has had his ethics— a social conscience with a moral auditory nerve which responded to the finest shadings of injustice. Writing with the intense Christian fervor of a Leo Tolstoi, Thoreau says in "Civil Disobedience," "Is there not a sort of blood shed when the conscience is wounded?"

Thoreau was an opposer: he was against society, slaves, institutions, church and politics; and the sum of his giant negations is a more illuminating text for a way toward understanding the subtler courtesies and gentler urges of men than those weedy and unkempt affirmations in Whitman's *Democratic Vistas*. The "canting peal" of Sunday morning service was as raucous to his ethical senses as the sound of an air-biting drayman's whip was to the ears of Schopenhauer. "I am too high-born to be propertied," he said. Announcing his total disallegiance to organized government, he wrote: "Know all men by these presents, that I, Henry Thoreau, do not wish to be regarded as a member of any Incorporated Society which I have not joined." To him the body politic was "covered with scoriae and volcanic cinders, such as Milton imagined."

Should we mistake this anger for misanthropy, we wholly misconceive Thoreau, for his virtues were heady enough; it was nature in him that was so diluted. He might do all within his abilities to ameliorate man's condition, his poverty and judgment and humble life in this world, but he could not stop loathing his low mortal habits. But he had ample goodness and urgently wanted on occasions to be easily familiar with the rhythm of habit, usage and ordinariness. We must curse the heavens for Thoreau's limits, for they were beyond correction.

Thoreau could say that the "utterer of oaths must have honeyed lips," sadly surmising that his own were so niggardly clothed. He could write, "There is no remedy for love but more love," without being able to love anyone. In one line—"I am not above being used, ay, abused, sometimes,"—he makes us his subjects; for he who can so trust life lives forever after. We see this long-nosed and thewy

New Englander with flinty eyes walking through Concord village, hoping that the meanest man, "Sam" the jailer, will call after him: "Thoreau, are you going up the street pretty soon? Well, just take a couple of these handbills along and drop one in at Hoar's piazza and one at Holbrook's, and I'll do as much for you another time." "There is some advantage in being the humblest, cheapest, least dignified man in the village, so that the very stable boys shall damn you."

Thoreau belonged, if he belongs anywhere, with the Christian anarchists of the world, with the Nazarenes, the Mennonites, the Dukhobors, with Tolstoi, although he lacked the Christian, tragic impulse that made Melville, Keats, Shakespeare and Tolstoi sit in Job's sackcloth and enact in their own lives the eternal Passion Play at the tomb of man's misery. *Walden* is the nearest he ever came to the drama of man. It is the drama of Fortitude succored by Logic, without any hidden trap doors of the heart. *Walden*, because it is so untouched by miscreeds, casts a dry light upon the Bible socialists of the Forties and Fifties, the era of the American communitarians: the Oneidans led by John Humphrey Noyes, Yankee apostle of pietism, socialism and complex marriages; the Rappites, shrewd colonizers and communistic economists, and "God-propped"; the Owenites of New Harmony, the Brook Farmers, the Shakers. Here we had, perhaps, the prefiguration of a Democratic America, the individual emancipated from State hegemony, or living apart, State-free. "If a State is governed by the principles of reason, riches and honors are the subjects of shame; if the State is not governed by the principles of reason, riches and honors are the subjects of shame." So wrote Confucius and so believed Thoreau. Thoreau was concerned only with the Orphic politics of the soul, the only politics for man—no politics. Character must sculpt its own background and Fate, and emit its own historical aureole.

This seer, whose body is fog, fen and vapor, was as subtle as the modern *diaboliques* of the flesh, as an Emile Verhaeren or a D.H. Lawrence. Thoreau feared conscience as much as evil; too much conscience bleeds the soul to death, and too much morality cankers the whole man. Thoreau eschewed all doctrine and all saviorism. Whitman's humanitarian bathos, his democratic rhodomontade —"I will not exclude you until the sun excludes you,"— was wholly alien to that quieter individual.

A visionary democrat, Thoreau was not too democratic, not too common, nor too clean. Thoreau was not the Common Man, although he reverenced what is innocent and humble in man and in himself. He wrote that Emerson was not "comprehensive" enough to trundle a wheelbarrow. He, of course, could build a fence, caulk a boat, hoe potatoes, although he made no occult humbug of the homespun agrarian life. When the triviality and dust of Concord galled him and he had to refresh his olfactories, he retired to Walden, picked the "hairy huckleberry" at Truro, fished, trekked through Maine, or lived with the Indians; and when he grew weary of all these changes he returned to Concord. Henry Thoreau had a sane imagination; he saw how great was the fall from man to farmer. Thoreau would have had no patience or sympathy with an Occidental cult of industry: in *Walden* he writes with a sententious tartness: "Why should they eat their sixty acres, when man is condemned to eat only his peck of earth?" Here again he was close to Tolstoi who said: "The exaltation of work is as monstrous as would be the exaltation of eating to the rank of a virtue."

He never wrote any fig and nut homiletics on the un-mitigated beatitudes of the life of the American Farmer, or, like Hector St. John de Crèvecoeur, turned America into an exotic Bible land of wild bees, maize, snakes and Indians. Thoreau never saw any vestal fires rise out of manure composts. He was so singularly without doctrine that he could write an essy, "Life Without Principle," and no conscientious reader could conceivably garble his meanings. He went wherever life sent him and made no credo of his private experience. He recorded it beautifully, and, if we have eyes, we can profitably read it and then pursue our own private follies, tinctured by his.

Walden itself is not a Manual of Conduct, but a mood, a Chanticleerian ode. Thoreau lived and sang it and, when he grew tired, he entirely forsook it. "I lived there two years and two months. And at present I am a sojourner in civilized life again." Elsewhere he writes in the same simple, unswollen vein: "I am naturally no hermit, but might possibly sit out the sturdiest frequenter of the bar-room, if my business called me thither."

He was too alert, and, with what irony we must confess it, too *dry* for the general pitfalls of men and the herd cures that each generation prescribes for itself. In this spirit he wrote about literature, democracy and America, jotting down rare observations, and offering no nostrums, "those quack vials of a mixture dipped from Acheron and the Dead Sea." Thoreau tells us that he liked a "tawny grammar"; relished a phrase that had the fiber and woody odor of sturdy hickory. But he never ruralized English or speciously Americanized it. He could write preternaturally exquisite passages on New England soil, grass, berry, In-dian relic, swamp, tarn or tare, without making a fetish of locale. "I wish," said Thoreau, "to get the Concord, the

Massachusetts, the American, out of my head and be sane a part of every day."

When we read Thoreau we no longer misconceive democratic literature. Thoreau's prose has the astral fragrance of dawn, an early "morning prescience" rather than the hue and emanation of apotheosized place. He is a Vulcan hammering out of lichen, maple, alder, sumac and berry, the purest essences of truth. His "Musketaquid" flows through those remote mountainous regions of the inward man.

There is Thoreau's New England—the soil, fertilized with the arrow and flint and immaculate bone of Indian and American Farmer—that he revered. There, fronting the Atlantic, are the severe weather shingles, skeletal remains of puritan bigotry and beauty, transfigured by sun and apricot blossoms into human flesh. There! Albert Pinkham Ryder's charred fumes of waves illuminated by mineraled moonlight.

Thoreau is the parable which will never be experienced until America has transmuted the logic of *Walden* into the lore of the heart. Keats has said, "Shakespeare led a life of Allegory: his works are comments on it." There is no other way of seeing *Walden*, ourselves, America, at this fevered moment.

One Oriental has suggested that if you take out the names and places in *Walden* it reads like a Chinese masterpiece; and it is true that we think of Henry David Thoreau as an Eastern sage; for the thought, vines, leaves and herbs of *Walden* are laved in the summery winds of the Vedas. Thoreau himself said, "The pure Walden water is mingled with the sacred water of the Ganges." From the Brahmans Thoreau learned patience, how to sit and wait, and, so needfully, how to be bored! Thoreau writes:

"Hippocrates even left directions how we should cut our nails." At the nethermost core of history, and at the underside of war and poverty, lies tedium. It is the grand malaise of the Western World. Europe today has a "crisis" every few weeks. It is the national flagellation which the dictators give to the wretched and the starving instead of bread. When Thoreau said that "the mass of men lead lives of quiet desperation" he read the funerary lines of Western man. How true it is that every little man, newspaper reader, shipping clerk, "rank and file" socialist and communist, cannot abide more notes, conferences and diplomatic parleys, not because he is so wicked and hypocritical, but because he needs a spurious, historical event, the pungent excitement of troop and fleet movement—another sexual dramatic "crisis" in the world—in his empty, slavish life—to save democracy and defend Soviet Russia! Is this exaggerated? A close reading of men's beliefs discloses that they do not emanate from the stars and heavens, from planetary ideas, but from the frenzied and agitated blood vessels. The exquisite poesy of carnage is at the root of the intellectual, the revolutionist, the student, the war correspondent, the fascist and the laborer. Look not at their principles but at the "nature" of them. Noble partisanship today has an undercrust of beast.

Since it is the mind that is the vessel of all good and evil in the world, why is it that we so distrust its strength in opposing the violence at large today. Thought is always prior to deed, war, history. Baudelaire said: "Every mind is a weapon loaded to the muzzle with will." However, never before have the seers of the world been so despised. And never before did Americans so need *Walden*. Is *Walden*, it is demanded, a system of economics, a doctrine, an organized panacea for social ills? It is none of these.

Walden is a vision; it is the "Bhagavad-Gita" of the moods and seasons of Conscience; it is a poet's rather than a law-giver's prayer. Conscience is various, brooding and chameleon, and is not a law any more than are the works of Shakespeare or Keats. Teach men to understand one single line out of *Measure for Measure* or the "Odes" and you teach them all they need and can ever know of the fervor of beauty which is the poetic ecstasy of justice. *Walden* is such a fervor and such an ecstasy. Know it, and none will raise his hand against another, none will be poor and none go to war.

"Justice," "beauty," "moral fervor," "ideals,"—are these not taboo words out of the unclean and stupid mouths of the unproselytized Gentile, the bourgeoisie? We live today in an age of foolproof certitudes. We ask, has Thoreau a theory, has this thinker an economic meta-physic? We have constructed out of economic theories an Atropos-like dogma, an iron fate, that is as certain to slay our minds and bodies as will the evils it is to correct. Man must eat, but must man eat man to have his loaf of bread? Can a bread and butter culture sustain society? Can ideal-ism be held, historically, in abeyance, while men murder for food—for ideals? Is there not a grim and baleful con-tradiction here; for there is more than one kind of feeding for mankind. "Woe be to the generation," wrote Henry David Thoreau, "that lets any higher faculty in its midst go unemployed!" Let us take care that the bread men get may not be the offal from Circe's sty. For man cannot *afford*, as he is doing, to neglect the chivalry of ethics in his pursuit of economic salvation. His *hunger* in the end will be so great, his denial so desperate, that he will break out in more bloody fury than before to reclaim his spirit; for spirit is so good and so evil and so chemic that, if you starve it, man will *eat* the whole world to have it back again!

But how can we overcome evil in the world, or can we? We have drifted far, far from the simple Christian logic of humanity: "Thou shalt not kill." We believe we are wiser, but we are only craftier. We know how to meet our enemy on his own terms: tank for tank, bomb for bomb. That is all. Thoreau with his face toward the East wrote: "The Brahmans never proposed courageously to assault evil, but patiently to starve it out." Men who see, see slow. The Buddha sits with his knees ruminatively folded under himself and waits; and the Occidental never learns the true vision of this posture. The wise Buddha waits upon history so that it can unfold itself in its own time; waits upon evil which must live its own life and die its own death. The Buddha patiently teaches and lets life do the rest.

Is this fatalism? We are fatalists only when we cease telling the truth, but, so long as we communicate the truth, we move ourselves, life, history, men. There is no other way. This is the simple epitome of the wisdom of nonresistance to evil. It is what Confucius, Thoreau and Tolstoi taught. It is the incredible, the visionary way, and it announces treason and betrayal more boldly than fire-arms or airplanes. Tolstoi, who deeply saw the virtue of comprehending simple things simply, answered the sophists who garbled his words: "All this apparently complicated proposition about non-resistance to evil and the objection to it reduces to this, that, instead of understanding it, as it is written, 'Do not resist evil or violence with evil or violence,' they understand (I even think, intentionally) that it says, 'Do not resist evil, that is, be indulgent to evil, be indifferent to it': whereas to resist evil is given as a rule how to struggle in the most successful manner against evil. It says, 'You are in the habit of struggling against evil by means of violence, or of retribution. This is a bad, a wicked, means.'"

We had in Thoreau's own time the Hopedale commune, the gentle Oneidans, the Harmonites, all of whom warmed over their socialisms with the Sermon on the Mount. We have as an immortal lesson in truth the way of the Christian Dukhobors of the Caucasus who refused to submit to military service and who burnt their weapons lest they be tempted to resist injury with violence. So powerful was the spirit of these meek Dukhobors that the Cossacks who guarded and whipped them had to be sent away because in the end they refused to do either. These are among the rare conquests of humanity.

The reason that we forget our true spirits so readily is that there is no frailer phantom, spun of such seraph-breathed tissue, than faith. Men require dogmas to support their eternally expiring beliefs. Great lives are moral allegories and so soon become deniable myths because we cannot believe that such good men could have existed in such an evil world. So we doubt the existence of Christ, the authorship of *Hamlet*, the profound human heart logic of Tolstoi, the miracle and wonder of *Walden*. But *Walden* does exist and for us. It is a revelation of the inward unity of the man that the beginning of *Walden* is on poverty and the conclusion on war. Show man that life at its apex is a supreme allegory and he will memorize *Walden* to the last syllable of its pulse. But persuade and hint. *Walden* cannot be rushed into men's hearts. "The light," says Thoreau on the final page of *Walden*, "which puts out our eyes is darkness to us. Only that day dawns to us to which we are awake."

III

RANDOLPH BOURNE:
IN THE SADDLE OF ROSINANTE

*For Alfred Stieglitz (1865-1946) who danced before
Art in a white stole, like David at the Ark.*

Look at Shakespeare's true men, Thersites and the Fool in *Lear*—garbed in such low and base bodies. To these belonged the deformed but inwardly transfigured hunchback, Randolph Bourne. His voice was as raucous to the ELDERS of the day as the fierce and pitchy outburst of the Fool in *Lear*:

> Truth's a dog must to kennel; he must be
> whipped out when Lady the brach may
> stand by the fire and stink.

Some faces speak out their direful truths. We have had three or more true and terrible countenances, the "ugly" Henry David Thoreau, Herman Melville cast in impenetrable frost, and the gnome Randolph Bourne. Truth is so repellent because it wears the lazar clothes of the world. Thersites can lie down beside Christ and Dostoevski. The scurvy Thersites, the gruesome flesh wounds of Christ and the harried crucifixes in the face of Dostoevski come from a most common and tragic sore—MAN. We see this parable of the terror of truth—truth twisted by the world it must perforce inhabit—in the encounter between Randolph Bourne and Theodore Dreiser.

In 1918 on a snow-flurried evening in front of the Night Court at Tenth Street, a large brooding man met a hapless dwarf wrapped in a black witch's cape and hat, and he sidled to the brick wall to let it pass. Ashamed of his fright he walked and meditated with darksome remorse upon man's pitiless reactions to a lamed man. Then he dismissed it from his mind until the same little figure came to his door and announced himself as Randolph Bourne.

The spirit of Bourne is revealed in Arthur G. Dove's drawing from James Earle Fraser's death mask. Here is the final text which life itself cannot contradict—the head is so Homeric and dramatic in its size that it seems to have wasted the body. Randolph Bourne had found, through what hurts and chagrins, a gay hauteur toward his physical limits. Waldo Frank writes that his aberrations were "rather the stigmata of some miscarried loveliness." Are we not all deformities, as Amiel has said, laboring to become angels?

Two books that he wrote, *The History of a Literary Radical* and *Untimely Papers*, both fragments and posthumously published, are remembered. *Untimely Papers* is the tomb where Randolph Bourne ate his last sorrowing bread among the war jackals of America. Radical emotion and philosophy had left profound marks upon Randolph Bourne. Whitman's *Leaves of Grass* and the anarchism of Peter Kropotkin had leavened his temperament; the writings of John Dewey had made ineradicable grooves in his nature. But finally he had to reject all credos and causes.

Wherever Bourne turned during the First World War for the balsam for his own lonely vision, he found this infernal screed: the Cause had eaten the man. Peter Kropotkin, who had thirsted like a Karamazov for those artesian springs of love, brotherhood and Christian pity, became a prowar anarchist! John Dewey had announced the "anti-septic war," and Thorsten Veblen had reviled the conscientious objector. We see history monotonously unfold its own serpent form. "Universal History is Monotony," said the German historian Ratzl. Now again we are in the Fifth Act of the man-eating tragedy, and the same Maenads are about to tear us limb from limb; we are making ready to go to war to heal the "nails in the wounds."

Randolph Bourne saw that the *homo economicus*, the "ideational automaton," was the result of the cult of politics. Man's demon, from Plato's dour and Mosaical *Laws* and *The Republic*, through Marx and Lenin, is politics. The cruelest hoax of communist teaching is the submergence of the individual identity into the herd will of the fatherland. There is no modern jest comparable in its baseness and cant to the one that demands the mutilation of the individual, his desires, will, reason, body and heart, for the sake of the social organism. To each man who craves breath, memory, bread, stars, moon and earth, his one and only living truth is: "I AM SOCIETY." Rend the flesh of any one of these personal, unique and celebrated I's, place ONE in chains, in prison or on the rack, and you bleed the consciousness of Man. Society rests upon this towering I, and the very holiness of life lies in the truth that the parts are greater than the whole.

Bourne's "Unfinished Fragment on the State" is the story of the Fall of the American Mind in the WAR; no American has indicated as Bourne did the absolute hiatus between the State and the nation. State history and the traditions of the people ravel contrariwise. The history of George Washington, Daniel Webster, Henry Clay, and that of Henry David Thoreau, Herman Melville and Walt Whitman have two distinct meanings, purposes and cycles. The Mexican War, *Walden*, *Moby Dick*, and the Battle of

Shiloh occur within two different spheres. While the Leviathan Democracy was eating Mexican Territory, Moby Dick was feeding on creamy patches of brit and saturnine eternities in the Pacific sea wastes. The two Leviathans are as historically remote from one another as Thermopylae is from *Faust*.

State emblems, functions, architecture, Capitol Hill and Grant's Tomb are glyphs of silence; States have no memories. The power of the State lies in the majesty of oblivion, in crypts, catafalques and mausoleums: in vaults where the remains of the Presidents, i.e., those sacral ciphers of public chronicles, evoke no tears and no laments. The canonical death-monuments of James Madison, John Quincy Adams, Grover Cleveland are bureaucratic commemoration odes. "The vanity of Monuments hath often obscured true graves," wrote Sir Thomas Browne, "and Cenotaphs confounded Sepulchres."

The canting stones of the State lie upon and seal the speech of the nation. The ghost of John Brown, the wailing apparitions of the innocent Haymarket Anarchists, Parsons, Spies and Engle, and the noble blood of Sacco and Vanzetti, like the shades of the Homeric underworld, cry for speech and memory; and only the nation can succor them. For the State cannot abide their remembrance. "A state is called the coldest of all cold monsters. Coldly it lieth also; and this lie creepeth from its mouth: 'I, the state, am the people,'" said Nietzsche.

The indivisible separation between the State and the people is made clearly manifest by the visible military and the police. Troops and police always stand between the president, the senator, the governor, the mayor and the people, even when the latter is applauding them. For the State and the people are indivisibly two. The lives, the occupations and the lore of the people are told in simple homely epitaphs in graveyards, but the chronicles of the State, like the Place Vendome obelisk, are made out of the cannons of Austerlitz. "War is the health of the State," wrote Nietzsche, but the health of the nation is peace, art, marriage, work and play. War is a State affair. The people do not make wars, they only lose them. Whether the State is the conqueror or the vanquished, the people are invariably the defeated; for the fate of the State is the nemesis of the people. Witness the sufferings of the French workmen and the peasants during the triumphal Napoleonic wars, or remember the conduct of the "republican" Thiers who so ignominiously beseeched Bismarck to use the Prussian troops that had violated the life and soil of France to suppress the Parisian communards! Enemy States have a deep common logic and are more in accord with one another than they are with their respective subjects.

"War is the health of the State." The attempt to elevate the State into godhead, savior, first cause, is but another stratagem to canonize plunder, war, theft, property and law. The conflict between the State and the church is the struggle for the pre-emption and the guardianship of first principles. The State cannot fulfill its rites and destiny without causal sanction. This is the meaning of the New State Passion Play and the mystery of the visionary *condottiere*, with the cloven gargoyle brow and the sorrowing Christly eyes, who prepares the nation for another GOL-GOTHA: ARMAGEDDON!

The survival of the State depends upon the most venal contradictions. Helen will not be ravished until her unspeakable beauty becomes a fragrant rumor throughout the world; and the State cannot ravage honor, justice, life and property without first making a proclamation of their inviolability. State authority, spoliation, war, and the "hallowed" markets rest upon Christian and Bible sanction. The theocratic Pilgrim Fathers of our American Genesis, no less than the Patriarchs, Abraham, Isaac and Jacob, knew the mystical ecstasy of the GRAPE, the LAND and the HOUSE. The American Constitution was framed by men whose appetite for property and land found a holy precedent in the Old Testament so earthily redolent of cattle, pasture, wool and fruit. The poor, equally as religious, could but sweeten their drudgery upon these imaginary sun-sloped vineyards and fruitlands.

The Constitution, as Bourne wrote, was a *coup d'état* against the people; the cordwainer, the mechanic, the farmer, the Common Man, disfranchised by the American Constitution, was a "democratic" Ishmael. Like the profane issue of the master Abraham and his servant Hagar, he was born out of hallowed wedlock and left to wander through the world, a wild man of affliction, accursed of men. The history and fable of American Democracy are best rendered in the words of Ratzl, "In the beginning was the ground rent."

Not since Thoreau has any American save Randolph Bourne shown such lucid anger against the mummery of the State. The State myth continues, nourished by doctrine, gospel and leaders. Pragmatism, socialism, trade unionism and communist statutes lead to state idealism. What hope is there in this slavish, self-cozening instrumentalism? Is there a Gideon here with pitchers and trumpets to rout Philistia? The State, the Tower of Babel, which Jehovah destroyed by confounding the tongues that there might be diverse races, is the logarithmic "classless society" of one speech, one culture, one international

Babel-Fatherland in which ideals shall be shibboleths, and the spirit the flag of Bread. It is this abject herd craving for universal unity which is, as Dostoevski wrote in "The Grand Inquisitor," the chief misery of mankind.

What upheavals of grief this false Banner of Bread has brought to man: little wonder that the famished city pleb, the students, the Spartacists, the socialist peasants of Germany and Russia, are the drowned clot of seed out of which the State Loaf has been kneaded! The Whore who sits upon the waters in the Apocalypse is the man-eating Dictator who leers, *"Freiheit und Brot!"* The MAN QUESTION is still in dark limbo, outside of time and history —like the griefs and tears of the dead in the *Inferno.* There it will remain, as Tolstoi said, "as long as we allow ourselves to be guided by an external authority, be it that of Moses and Christ for one man, that of Mohammed for another and that of the socialist Marx for another." Doctrinaire guides, Martin Luther, Marx, Lenin, have been State idealists, the great man-eaters in history. Lenin promised that the State would eventually wither away, but nay, it is not the State but the people that wither away.

All dogmas lead men to the Abyss; doctrine is the enemy of vision and the denial of the past. This is what Bourne meant by "the new orthodoxies of propaganda." The ideologue seals up the history of mankind so that his acts can be State-chronicled from a new year One. Rifle man of the reminiscences of the race and you enslave him. Without memory man is a most rueful and fumbling creature, coerced to dwell in the dungy cave of the Cyclops.

Thoreau tried to teach us and himself to live, act and react without principles; he apprehended the true meaning of John Brown. He could defend and speak out for that heretic without losing his own soul and instincts in

the despotic tyranny of any heresy. What need had he or we of a credo to feel? If injustice, meanness and degradation do not make the blood mount in torrents of anger, in indignation, do not make the flesh and organs tremble in upreaching wrath, then screeds and cults will not avail either!

We cannot pity or love or be MAN save in the Topheth of our remembering bones. For what are our avowals and covenants unless our blood and bones acknowledge them, aye, remember them, when we cower and hide! Do we need a credo to comprehend Proudhon's "Property is theft"; do we require a set of principles to declare that war is slaughter, hate, rapine; must we have articles of faith to be free? Creeds have a way of taking their revenge upon us; the sanely thirsting instincts that do not have happy and untutored expression become manic and destroy their owners. Look at our early peace-cult Quakers who became the most gory whalers in America. Consider the dogmatic radical who has eaten the teachings of Marx like primitive tribes devour their sacred totems. It is the destroying satanism of his "revolutionary" will that moves him; he will pillage, burn, purge, dismember to safeguard the totemic Doctrine that will save man!

Bourne did not believe that another Armageddon would bring hapless man the final peace. War, he knew, like the mighty seed of Abraham, will beget war in ceaseless succession. Bourne envisaged the holy purifications of an entire people at peace, a nation withstanding the Juggernautic State, a people baptized in peace, while a world was occupied in destruction. What rare bursting *élan*, what warming miraculous humanities might not come from men who had tasted quiet? Here was one of those illimitable destinies beyond all realistic imaginings. But it was not to be. There was and is an ominous apathy to peace. The Caliban-like lethargy of American labor, of the present-day radicals, is a portent and peril to the people. The apostles of violence have given the septic kiss to the State and covertly await the DAY, even as their enemies do. Were they even true militants of revolutionary coercion, they would go into the pulsing streets of every city and industrial center and enact the unspeakable horror of the hydra, WAR, just as the English troupe used to do as it went from one hamlet to another with the Passion Play. They would inculcate the General Strike and organize with syndicalist imagination guerrilla strikes in every town to destroy the mysticism of the State, to re-create the people, and to make them ready for their own odyssey.

Randolph Bourne, who was a radical by temperament —for he could not bear inhumanities, had small faith in the "revolutionary" Marxist or in the American pragmatist. He called himself an IMPOSSIBILIST, a ridiculous word to the multitude. Few men will hazard envisaging themselves in ludicrous postures. The niggard limits which the pragmatist imposes upon his questions betoken a fear of speculation. It is upon this Rock of Fear that the American prophets of expediency, the radical and the pragmatical minds, have flogged the people.

Bourne was a Quixotist not yet come into his own; he saw that MAN is the end. Man is so noble to the Quixotist that even if he be set upon the most pathetic jade, he will tower against the mountainous skies. The propagandist, however, so bemoans forlorn man that he will not acknowledge him until he is multiplied a millionfold into the abstract MASS MAN. In the trifling dogma that places society above man there is a loathing and fear of the inside man (what then is this squeamish bias for the extrovert) and a warranty that man is not the end but the ghastly means toward some transhuman goal.

Imagine how despicable that low, comic mortal, Don Quixote, mounted on Rosinante and armored with a pasteboard visor to do battle for love, brotherhood and peace, must appear to the scientific extrovert. Imagine this poor Quixote, with "windmills in his brain," hoping to conquer man without bombs, poison gas and air raids!

Bourne conceived such homely and radiantly mortal errors; this was his desperado impossibilism, and for this we remember him. We recall him to guide us, as Vergil led Dante from one fiery circle to another, through the infernal limbo of American Culture where Thoreau, Melville, Whitman still clamor for the ripe, warm light of this world. Bourne loved our master spirits and he wanted to reclaim them for us who need them so profoundly. But now, such is the grim and repetitious fate of our men of truth, Randolph Bourne, too, lies in oblivion and is as unknown as our own tradition. We turn our back upon our own past as though it were as horrible to behold as Medusa. Would we but cease bemoaning our youth and see what we have, we might, like Saul, the son of Kish, who went out to seek his father's asses, find a kingdom!

IV

CAN THESE BONES LIVE

" 'Son of man, can these bones live?'
'O Lord God, Thou knowest.' "

A Lated Tribute to Ford Madox Ford:
How often since the Fates made you the
companion of Saul, David, Empedocles,
Maria Rilke, D. H. Lawrence, have I descended into Hades to converse with you.
Though the deceased wail in pitiless Orcus,
our moan is the sharper, because we who
live dwell alone and unsure in the cragged
eyries and mountain fastnesses of a defiant
solipsism. How solitary our own earth-heart
is, cheated, but yesterday, of these tumult-
ing Images who gave us speech and
memory, as did the libations of blood
poured forth by Odysseus. Aye, we are the
poor, maimed shades, Sir!

As I deeply bow to place my lips upon
your Brow, in gratitude for your Grace and
dispensations to me, I weep because my
homage is the coarse and pusillanimous
thanks of the living to the dead. My pardon
and my sorrow, Kind Genius, Good, Savory
Ford Madox Ford.

1. ISHMAEL

There has been no more clinkered land for the artist to live in than America. All artists, everywhere, are pariahs. However, some countries gravel them the more, and so hinder their fates that their lives, like the three throats of Cerberus, are brutishly peeled. Maxim Gorki, uttering his own apprehensions and love, wrote that as long as Leo Tolstoi was upon the earth he was not an orphan. In darkest Russia the disenchanted saints and demons sometimes saw and aided each other; spoke one to the other upon their trembling veins. But so apart and incommunicable have been our own poets that we search for letters, for buried mementos and fragments of conversations to disclose whether Herman Melville had even heard of *Leaves of Grass*, whether Poe and Melville had met or whether *Moby Dick* was known to the Brahmans. Could there be a more melancholy concealment than the verse of Emily Dickinson, hid in the domesticated sarcophagus of a drawer—"snug in seraphic cupboards." Follow this parable of the tomb in Edgar Poe, whose charnel passion for spectral and interred manikins—Berenice, Eleonora, Ligeia—Lady Ligeia!—reminds us of the sense-bereaved and starved girl who caresses and lips the doll in Gorki's short story.

Puritanism sundered men from one another. Henry James, the old maid of Puritan irregularities, of *comme il faut* peccadilloes, said that "introspection, thanks to the want of other entertainment, played almost the part of a social resource." When our pilgrims met in town house or for devotionals, each was celled, or pew-ed, theologically or politically, in the atom of his godhead. The white hygienical church, no less than the sabbatical cerements, the Sunday suit, was an altar and a garb for stern Jehovah and not for feeble and bemoisted man.

Consider in this light the long immurement of Herman Melville; he had not a soul to turn to, save Pilgrim Nathaniel Hawthorne, who in the "polar privacies" of his journals tells us that Herman Melville's linen was none too clean! Obviously, that healthful adhesiveness that Whitman prayed for could not be there. Melville needed human friendship. Hawthorne hovered over Herman Melville as a wraith, as Melville's own monody suggests. Raymond Weaver, author of *Herman Melville, Mariner and Mystic*, says that the apparitional face in *Pierre* is Hawthorne's. Yet the Pittsfield companionship between the sea-faring Triton, who had kneaded a vision of the night out of *Lear*, *Timon*, Ezekiel, Job and the magical jetting sperm of the leviathan, and the artistic Puritan from Salem was meager.

Van Wyck Brooks has said that Herman Melville was so lonely he dedicated *Pierre* to Mount Greylock and *Israel Potter* to the Bunker Hill Monument. But inviolably alone as Melville was, he did not perish unto himself; he but died to America. Nor did Poe. Poe's flight into the snowy steppes of metaphysics, to "Eureka," was an act of imaginative will. The true artist never disintegrates; he might fail, as Poe did in "Eureka," as Melville did in

Pierre, but, ah, so to fail! Or he might woo silence and darkness as Herman Melville did, eating his piece of limbo for two decades and more as an obscure custom house inspector on Gansevoort Street.

There is no more miserable fable than the one that suggests an early dissolution of Melville's vestal fires, the dying out of the Etna of his imagination. There is a herd reason in those critics who try to prove that the artist almost invariably surrenders to Success. Thoreau, Poe, Melville did not. Melville wrote, "All fame is patronage, I want to be infamous." Six months before his death in his seventy-second year, he completed the short novel, *Billy Budd*, almost as original as *The Piazza Tales*, also buried—"Alms for oblivion."

Ugly, bald dirt, as though cast down his ghostly gullet, lies upon Herman Melville. He is in Woodlawn Cemetery, that PIT OF ACHERON betwixt the subway terminus and the hither fringes of Yonkers, cankered with graying curls of dust from the yards of monument makers and palled with bitter macadam and the orchidaceous fumes of automobile gasoline. Is it not fitting, so American, that the most astonishing genius that ever came out of the Western Hemisphere should be so uncleanly slabbed in mean, cheap dirt, not among the pitiable poor, but with the common drab bulk of rightly unremembered dead. Look upon his sparse tombstone and read the frugal inscription written thereon, "OCCUPATION WRITER"; then utter aloud the pity for the artist, that Hamlet so dolorously sighs forth before his father's apparition, "Alas! Poor Ghost."

Our artists are American Ishmaels doomed to be cut away from the human vineyard. "Call me Ishmael," prophetically utters Herman Melville in the first line of *Moby Dick*. We are brute, giant pathfinders, without a remembrance of the past or tradition, discoverers of brand-new nostrums for sex, life, science, art and religion. We are the infant aboriginals. Before Poe, who? Before Whitman, Dreiser or Sherwood Anderson, who? Dreiser, like Cyclops after his one eye has been gouged out by the axle of Odysseus, blindly stumbles into truths, or into crowd folklore. We are iconoclasts who demolish Revelations, all mystery, doubt, confounding legends—to have what? Rousseau's *Social Contract*, Thomas Paine's *The Crisis*, Robert Ingersoll's arid-pated atheism, instead of the errors of Job, Daniel and Luke? Like that gross jackanapes in *The Idiot*, we have put the mouse behind the grate that it may nibble upon the icon Virgin Mary; and after the Image has been gnawed by the atheistical mouse, what remains? No poets were ever so arrogant as the American. The earth-gods, while serving as humble, common journeymen, word-cobblers, image-weavers, prayed that the soul of a Master might descend upon them; Shakespeare learned from Marlowe, Job, Plutarch, Ezekiel; Gogol issued from Pushkin, and Dostoevski from both.

How moving is Elisha's entreaty to Elijah that a double portion of his Master's Spirit fall upon him; "Thou hast asked a hard thing," replies the dying Elijah. When the noble Prophet rises in a chariot of fire, Elisha, weeping for the Mantle of Truth of the departing one, cries out: "My father, my father, the chariot of Israel and the horsemen thereof!" How else can a humble, aye, vast heart weep for his gifts! How then, lest we be gorged with our fathers, as Maria Rilke spoke, can we know that less than little that is to be understood?

Plato, who writes again and again that knowledge is reminiscence, has Socrates say: "What would you not give

to converse with Orpheus and Musaeus and Hesiod and Homer?" It assaults and pierces us to prayer when Odysseus descends into Hades to capture the flittering presence of his venerable mother: thrice he tries to take hold of her image: thrice she flies out of his hands. This is what the Greek Poets and Dante meant by transmigration, which is that reverend pilgrimage into other souls.

Foreknowledge is the rear of memory; prophecy in Shakespeare is the warm and viable echo of Montaigne or Job; just as intuition in *Moby Dick* is often a visionary rekneading of *Lear, Hamlet, Timon.* One book may empower a poet: Revelations was the polestar of Emily Dickinson. With what humble homage Dostoevski cried: "Go down in the dust before Corneille!"

With a deep and reassuring remembrance of the poets that had gone before him, Whitman might have made the *Leaves of Grass* an Homeric utterance instead of a revivalistic chant of sex that too often recalls the rank and gaudy age that produced Henry Ward Beecher and Mary Baker Eddy. Walt Whitman, as Raymond Weaver has said, may have gone over to Plymouth Church for the yeasty pabulum of the *Leaves*. How close is the athletic, amative porousness of Whitman to Beecher, how intimately related it is to Mary Baker Eddy and to the celebrated "Battle Axe Letter" of John Humphrey Noyes. Europeans compose testaments, journals, poems, but we have to make a Genesis, a Democratic Hygiene. We set out alone, upon our own *native* intelligences, looking for an East Indies, and, alas, find only an America!

Take that other aboriginal of diabolism, Edgar Poe. He, like Whitman, had almost no past. Walt Whitman was the pioneer Cosmos, before him nothing. He was the innocent, aromatic arm-pitted Man before the great Pollution, the Fall, and Edgar Poe was the brand-new Adamic Evil, the original serpent in the Garden. Poe had to invent everything because he remembered almost nothing. He was, as Van Wyck Brooks suggests, the American Edison of the black arts of sensation—a scientific shaman of *cauchemar* omens. A *ratskeller* Vulcan, Edgar Poe hammered out upon the stithy of his moaning soul little Gothic Petroushkas, mechanical horror dolls, Ligeia, Una and Monos.

By inheritance and birthright Poe possessed the most dread theme of man, evil. But he never got beyond the mechanics of devilism, the draperies gorged with the in-

censed stuff of decomposition, the death-battened cerements, the meretricious mystery of the immured groans.

Could Edgar Poe have spoken out of himself, out of remembered nature, as he does in the Letters pooled with anguishing tears and loneliness, he might have uttered a minor Faustian tragedy. He might have made a lovely, sensual Margaret, instead of lacquering seraphic and sepulchral manikins who utter ventriloquistic shudders, so like the much smaller Gothic "bioloquist" Charles Brockden Brown—lo, the "Father of the American Novel"!

The fetish of originality is our curse. Dante took a

guide! What a myth of Memory is the journey through the *Inferno* where the Poet sees, talks to and weeps with each smitten and hapless ghost.

Both Whitman and Poe have been accused of plagiarism; alas, it is an untruth. Traherne's mystic physic of love, joy and earthy stuffs, those prescriptive listings of towns, ships and wines, Whitman never knew. Walt Whitman never transcended Sir Walter Scott. Shakespeare, whom he had read but totally garbled, was but a "feudal poet" of the past, alien to his trembling democratic organs. Walt Whitman was never influenced by any poet. He was native, large, new, cosmical and ignorant. Edgar Poe's filchings were irrelevant and harmless. He had an obsession about plagiarism and attacked the Boston Brahmans as gross pilferers. Fortunate for them they had the canny wisdom to steal their truths, for they had little or none in their own loins. Imagine the aphorisms of Emerson without Plato, Shakespeare, Marcus Aurelius, Plutarch or Hegel.

Our true poets lived in the agony of their own sealed redoubts. Each one was an original Monad, uninfluenced by the other. The four or five spirits of the nineteenth century were only dimly aware of one another's existence. Whitman had met the "infamous" Poe once; Melville, we learn from an extant letter, had read the *Leaves*. What he thought is not known. Poor Emily Dickinson had heard rumors of a "scandalous" book by an author whose name was Walt Whitman. Her own verse, those chaste and holy privacies that have the odor of Juliet's whited tomb, was posthumously printed. Herman Melville was such a forgotten figure that an English admirer could not even find him. "How good to be safe in tombs," whispered Emily Dickinson.

2. SANCTIFIED LIES

We have not lacked poets but what we have most mournfully missed are critics. Herman Melville ceased writing, almost entirely, for forty years, because there was not one man in the whole of America to celebrate *Moby Dick, Pierre, The Piazza Tales.* Emily Dickinson in her solitude had to turn for appreciation to Higginson, the paunchy Presbyterian Silenus of Literature.

Poe's literary executor and biographer, Rufus Griswold, was his covert enemy. Read what puling venom that pen distilled in behalf of his deceased subject. Rufus Griswold hated Edgar Poe.

Edgar Allan Poe has had no critic save D. H. Lawrence. His Christian biographers and analysts approach him as some transmoral monster, who, unfortunately, had genius. Poe, they censoriously moan, drank; Poe took a child-wife; Poe took laudanum. Poe finally took his life in the gutters of Baltimore.

Look at our critics: George Edward Woodberry, Bliss Perry, Vernon Louis Parrington, W. C. Brownell, those doughty yeomen and sterile grammarians of American literature. They have been busily engaged, in the name of place and literary chauvinism, in setting up a little Baal of myth and history. Without eyes to see what we have, they fatten the leanest kine that have grazed upon our skinny Parnassus. They have given us a colonial renascence by exhuming William Dunlap, a "Father" of American Playwriting, Philip Freneau, the revolutionary versifier, and Charles Brockden Brown, a diminutive bogus demon. But poets comprehend themselves better than their critics, even trivial ones. Brockden Brown knew his wizened limits so much more acutely than his American

Cambridge resurrectors; he cremated his one play and deposited the ashes in his snuffbox!

The Whitman pietists are no better. Walt Whitman was surrounded by cultists—Dr. Bucke, George O'Connor, John Burroughs, John Addington Symonds and Horace Traubel —who came to the Democratic Pythagoras of sex, diet, hygiene, for tonical purposes. The *Leaves of Grass* for them was a laying on of hands. Walt Whitman, with the help of his starveling apostles, came near to becoming the Mary Baker Eddy of American Literature. Worse than the neglect of a poet is a churchly idolatry of his person. For he who oversanctifies Genius, like pathetic Peter at the crowing of the chanticleer, thrice denies him!

So we are still finding and losing Whitman. Today, many recoil from Walt Whitman. We are uncrossing ourselves before the Whitman shrine. The idol is broken and looks a little ridiculous. We suspect the Adamic floutings, the spinal manifestos. Still, the Nature Man, he of the Cosmic Phallic Aches, is not to go unremembered. The poet-evangelist who tried to break Plymouth Rock can never be forgotten.

The critical humbug continues, disguised as scientific or aesthetic or proletarian analyses of literature. There is no more boring or feckless hoax than the aesthetic-scientific vocabulary. If you would forevermore misread Shakespeare, Cervantes, Ben Jonson or John Keats, go to those homuncular gods, Croce, Kant, Bosanquet, I. A. Richards.

Criticism is an act of creative faith, and there is no historical approach that can ultimately disclose mummified secrets, sphinxed in time and place, that the naked eyes, the bones and the pulses cannot of themselves discover or apprehend. The critic who hides behind science is concealing NO-BODY. Criticism, painting, poetry, are but deeply awakened self-love. AMOR FATI means to love one's fate and truths, and he who does not love his own truths, absolutely, would be more truthful if he kept silent.

All is relative, murmurs the poltroon. True! Now that this is granted, have we not the right to demand what the critic feels and sees, Absolutely, in this tragic, fleeting and relative world? We thirst for the Absolute, as Dante anguished for Beatrice; that She does not exist has nothing to do with our hunger, love and pursuit of the infinite. We are all FOOLS, we pray, as Don Quixote was; let us not be ashamed and furtive about it, and slink behind the errors of science, philosophy or metaphysics.

So let us have done with the quackery of drab relativism; for the critic who cannot make the distinction between Melville and Poe and the Draculean satanism of Brockden Brown and William Faulkner, between Chartres and the pulp Gothics of the mortuary Chrysler Building, is a pusillanimous Philistine.

Away with the scientific, the proletarian and the psychoanalytic fraud in literature. Enough of the maundering truisms on poems and artists from the Poloniuses upon the Hamlets, from the Jungs, the Otto Ranks, the Plekhanovs, the Trotskys, the Marxists. Enough of this man is split, that poet is mad, and that novelist is class-conscious. What need had the artist to make himself whole, were he not split? Poe, like Lazarus, comes to us from the grave in each tale, poem and line.

After the "scientist" has pronounced a Nietzsche or a Proust a schizophrenic, what has he revealed? He has, to be sure, told us that he is a schizophrenic. It is the teachable and mundane truth that Polonius unlocked for us as

he held in the palm of his hand the quicksilver of Hamlet's
lunacy:

> Mad call I it; for, to define true madness,
> What is't but to be nothing else but mad?

What do the Marxian Poloniuses of class-conscious
literature disclose? What is proletarian literature? Why,
to utter simple truth, it is literature about the proletariat.
And who is this Neanderthal Pleb so wantonly chained
to his machine but a breathing, star-thirsting man, aye, so
we pray—a Man, a Volpone, an Iago, a Timon, a Job. There
is nothing else to it but that. He is the forlorn "featherless
biped" and there it is. Time has not changed him: love
has not, greed and stealth have not.

There is enough mystery and terror in this truth for any
poet. But then there is always the "scientist," not Empedocles or Heraclitus, those soothsayers of unguessed
dreams, but the kilometer critics who would weigh and
balance the pulse and beat of Job's sorrow upon his dunghill, who would capture the width, size and orbit of Ahab's
nature. Can there be a deeper image or a profounder
cetology than that which comes from the creamy brit
weaving upon the sea heaths where Moby Dick pastured?

We go to the critic, to Lessing or to Heinrich Heine, to be warmed in the wondrous Priapic fluids of his brain. As critics, their viable, "sanctified lies," as Nietzsche called art, have the same potencies that the stories of Greek mythology have given to man. We desire the same quickening from the critic that we have from the poet. *The Laocoön* and *The Birth of Tragedy* come from a kindred throb. Just imagine what girth the god or man or critic had who wrote that when the genital organ of Cronus, father of Zeus, struck the sea it created an enormous tidal wave in which Aphrodite was born.

The critic is the Sancho Panza to his master, our Lord Don Quixote, the artist. Sancho is no bread, butter and beer realist. He too sees and knows with the magical folly of the heart that there is knowledge before reason and science, a secret wisdom that is prior to logic—the vibrant god-telling PULSE. "There are reasons of the heart of which Reason knows nothing," said Pascal.

There are no abstract truths—no Mass Man, no proletariat. There is only Man. When the Pulse has been nailed upon the crossbeams, lo, Reason gives up its viable breath and becomes a wandering ghostly Error. Truth and folly are ever about to expire, so that we, like our beloved Sancho Panza, kneeling at the deathbed of Don Quixote, must always be ready to go out to receive the holy communion of cudgels and distaffs for the rebirth of the Pulse.

3. THE FLESH REFUSED

America for a hundred years was a vineyard. The Puritan feared and despised all the arts as coming from the nether, concupiscent soul; he transmuted his own needs and appetites into meditations and chronicles that were redolent of sod, vintage and flocks. His materialism was his shrine; he knelt in devotional adoration, not to the Virgin, Jesus or the Saints, but to the fields, the house, reverentially white, and the orchard. From Abraham, Noah and Job he derived the ecstasy and fervor he had for his sheep, apples, wood and grain. The colonial farm house, rooted in and winging upwards from the soil, bespeaks the miracles of growth, life, birth, procreation and marriage. The Puritan's churchly slaying of the sexual organs, like the dismemberment of Osiris, was a furtive and diabolical worship of seedtime, spring and copulation.

The Puritan walked and meditated with Orion, dog-wood, the birch, and he furtively knew the nakedness of his body as Ham knew Noah.

The sensual Puritan was wiser and also cannier than the artist. He slew witches, denounced devils, adultery and fornication, but commonly had five or more wives; the naïve Pilgrim artist accepted Jehovah, Calvin and America, and denied fleshly man.

Almost the whole of American Literature has been a deep refusal of man. Early American Literature, veiled in the lilied twilight of St. Matthew and St. Mark, is a death pilgrimage, a renunciation of the carnal heart. The very pulses of Poe, Emily Dickinson and Hawthorne desolately shake as in their own Gethsemane. O Calvary, Calvary, moaned Emily Dickinson. O Eureka, Ligeia, Death, wept Poe. "Man doth not yield himself to the angels, nor unto death utterly, save only through the weakness of his feeble will," wrote Poe, quoting Joseph Glanvill.

The flight from man and nature *begins* with Edgar Poe. Ligeia, Madeline and Berenice are moon-veined Juliets, and Eleonora has "memorial eyes" and a sarcophagus brow.

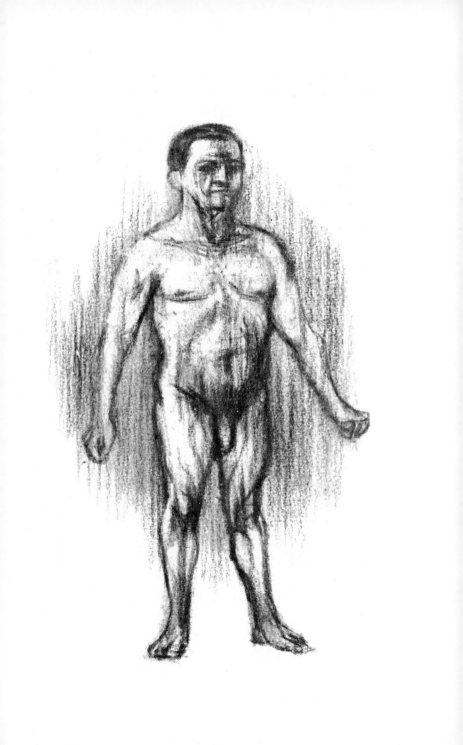

Herman Melville, the most corporeal artist of the American nineteenth century, was under the pall of the New Testament. Melville read his Shakespeare as a Sermon on the Mount; his last words and Epitaph, *Billy Budd*, is a Christian Hymn. Billy Budd, like Alyosha Karamazov, is Christly goodness; he is Innocence before the Adamic "mysteries of iniquity."

Hawthorne's men and women are aerial and epicene dews, like the tissueless seraphs of Simeon Solomon. There is no human pollution in any of his novels. His most evil pages distill an edenic miasma instead of rank protoplasm.

Our entire Christian literature is a sacral whiteness. Herman Melville wrote a whole chapter on WHITENESS. From Poe, Emily Dickinson and Hawthorne to the present-day painters and ghostly water colorists, we see this Parsifal Annunciation of White Death. Witness the immaculate vulva flowers of Georgia O'Keeffe, the bleached valley of death-shells, rams' skulls, lilies, and whited roses. Or see the total exclusion of the human face, not once the stigmata or the imprint of the fingers, the eyes, the flesh in Marsden Hartley's seascapes, dead birch logs and stones. Man lies hidden and secretly veined far underneath Hartley's aching brine-washed rocks and pulsing sublunary seas. The Face remains unguessed, as in Poe's tales, walled up in the sepulcher of stones, tools and breakers, or in the bloodless wash of sedge, marge or bay of John Marin's water colors. WATER COLOR, it is so deeply American!

What is the fetish of whiteness? What does this lusting after Hygeia mean? What else but the revulsion from one's own blood and the unholy dread of the *sub rosa* Unclean Man. Thoreau, who loathed man's low habits and looked upon eating, copulation or defecating as the vile

malady of mortals, wrote, "We are so degraded that we cannot speak of the necessary functions of human nature."

In almost a hundred years of American Literature we do not have one feeding, breeding, sexual male, not one suffering, bed-pining Manon Lescaut or a Shulamite. There are no ripe women here. Writes the poet William

Carlos Williams in *In The American Grain*, "Emily Dickinson, starving of passion in her father's garden, is the very nearest we have ever been—starving."

We have had spectral essences, odorless and hueless. What is *The Scarlet Letter* but a delicate aprioristic theorem of SIN. The evidence that Hester Prynne ever slept with little ether-blooded Dimmesdale is as etiolated and remote as the ontological proof of the existence of God in Aquinas's *Summa*. There is no anatomy at all in Puritan Literature. The illicit relation between Hester and Dimmesdale is a copulative dance of the Essences. Since our beginnings, we have had but one enormous Hymen Hymenee, one seminal marriage between male and female, and that is the nuptial of the leviathan who copulates upon the sweet April brit and grassy meadows of the ocean.

Aye, all essence. Edgar Poe hurried into the arms of Divine Essence, of Eleonora, Eureka, or Death, to appease his thwarted heart's pinings. The blasphemous kiss that Poets have put upon the wan cheeks of their metaphysical Beatrices or Ligeias we pardon because of the suffering denials of their lives. We moan with Poe and clasp his dear ghostly remains. But, as we descend into the underworld and pass the shade of Nathaniel Hawthorne, we move by with an oblique glance, for when he lived, he had but ghost corpuscles. Poe's diabolism was tragic, Hawthorne's, lilied. For our Last Supper of Memory we must have bread; dew, moss and sumac cannot feed our beatitudes or our grief.

We bury ghosts, Ligeia, Berenice, Eleonora, only to resurrect real cadavers, McTeague and Vandover. Refuse the bones and the worms as Hawthorne and Poe did and what is ultimately begotten is the contemporary underground biped, brain-spawn of the same flesh and bone denial. The exquisitely figurined Ligeia is sensually and humanly as nonexistent as the abstract cankered Outside Man. The ghosts, the phantoms, and the present-day economic bipeds are no-man.

Does not Tolstoi's Ivan Ilytch make his life upon this knowledge; at the abyss, before death, the provincial magistrate sheds himself as a generalized man. He renounces that conspiratorial Socratic syllogism that makes him man and mortal in consequence of an arithmetical and logical conjecture, that subtracts him from a frozen, throbless and metaphysical humanity. So long as Ivan Ilytch, the Socratic integer, despises himself and his sickness, he decomposes upon his tongue, breath and skin; the odor that steals out of his clothes and bed separates him from humanity, his family and himself. Christianity cannot help, Holy Writ is in vain—all is lost; there is no way back to the living save through the memory of his own organs. Ivan Ilytch vindicates his life, just before dying, not by a rationalistic subterfuge, but through the simple cleanly act of his servant who brings the bedpan to him and accepts this seemly necessity of nature in his sick master. Ivan Ilytch forgives his coarse family and children, and dies a Christian, because his peasant servant cannot make those distinctions between a man in his social and decorous clothes and in his honestly defecating necessities. Icons, candles, Christ, society and superstition cannot make a man a Christian but a bedpan can!

See what all the spirit-glutted souls, the rationalists and the ethical metaphysicians, who took to their apriori bosoms the remote abstract Mass Man—see what the spectral humanity-guzzlers have done.

All, from Plato, Immanuel Kant, Hegel, Emerson,

Thoreau, Hawthorne and Kropotkin, to the socialists and communists, have been adepts in the humanity cult. The brotherhood of man has always attracted men without adequate blood-pigmentation, like Kant and Thoreau, who arrive at the love of man through the multiplication tables and the categories. Both of these moral teachers had an egregious distaste for man. Kant kept himself closeted all his life in Königsberg because he would encounter fewer specimens of the genus, man. Thoreau, so earnest and truthful, ate a muskrat to overcome his flesh-revulsion. Immanuel Kant devoured the categorical imperatives instead, and neither the muskrat nor the categories helped.

But the end of rationalism is not its own abstractions, but carnal error, or blood-revenge, as Thoreau's orgiastic and savage refusal of the woman who had proposed to him, or Immanuel Kant's vile definition of marriage as "a treaty of reciprocal possession by the two parties which is made effective by the reciprocal use of their sex properties." Immanuel Kant embraced godhead, the universe, the abstract Man, and, as he himself confessed, masturbated! While Aristotle, Master of Schoolmen, as the story goes, crawled on all fours, his rider, not the Golden Mean, but his mistress flourishing a whip!

Purge the flesh and you canker the spirit. Christian rationalism and nature are forever at odds. Grapes and bread do not grow upon the Categories or upon Calvary. The Cross and the Categorical Imperatives but mock their hapless bearers. Whitman unsuccessfully tried to marry Saviorism and Eros. Although Whitman sang the most carnal hymns to the pagan body, he was really a teetotaler and an ascetic. He was a St. John the Baptist of sexual love; like all friars, artistic or Christian, Whitman took the veil, for life, for frugality, for sexuality, for man.

Our Americans, from Herman Melville, Whitman, John Humphrey Noyes, Henry Adams, Thorsten Veblen to Theodore Dreiser, have had the peculiar gift, native, no doubt, of annulling their deepest beliefs; like Penelope they weave their fates and then unravel them. So puzzled were Whitman's own disciples that they endeavored to prove to the American Public that the Master, who had preached the deep delights of the senses, had been himself a piously chaste male. That is an American riddle. Popes confound us because they had daughters, Walt Whitman befuddles us because he had none!

Resolve the riddle of the flesh made spirit and the ambiguities of Puritan literature dissolve. Otherwise, the tales, the novels and the poems seem to be but recondite craft. How much easier it is to know what Chekhov or Dostoevski felt or thought than it is to understand the demonology of Poe and Melville.

The Puritan failed as an artist and became an esoteric artificer; he created charnel-house dolls, an upboiling metaphysical sea, instead of a human comedy. His works are ecliptic, and his anonymity is a subterfuge art, a sacral lie. We cannot say that he was less gifted than the Europeans; for who can finally proclaim that the fires and the snows of Melville's Vesuvian brain are not to be compared with Dostoevski's. Imaginatively, he was the European master's peer; but as a Living Voice, infinitely less. We have had the most abstruse technicians in America, but never a Voice.

The Puritan signed away his flesh for Christ's bread as irrevocably as Dr. Faustus abjured his life to Mephisto for carnal pleasure. Here is the enigma of the disembodied literature of the Puritans: these Americans would not, dared not, wed the flesh and so espoused godhead. The

pursuit of the White Whale is the allegory of a disincarnate Ahab seeking after his own flesh. Although Herman Melville might create an unchristian Ahab to flaunt, "I do not baptize thee in the name of the Father, but in the name of the devil," the final text upon Melville's entablatured bones is the Sermon on the Mount. "How men lust after a piece of spirit," cried Nietzsche, "when a piece of flesh has been denied them."

Refusals beget deeper refusals. By the time we come to Henry Adams the American fable wondrously unfolds. Henry Adams was a timorous Bacchus, who revealed to the American that the Virgin of Chartres was the perfect Catholic Aphrodite. Later, however, he elevated Mary into pure juiceless intellection. Then he forswore the Virgin altogether and knelt at another shrine, the MACHINE, and so concluded his days in epicene sanctity, deriving unguessed erotical vibrations in his Gallery of Machines, from nine-foot pistons, lathes, belts and wheels. "The strain of man is bred out into baboon and monkey."

Here is the whole allegory of the Fall of Man in the American Garden of Eden. After Hester Prynne, after Ligeia and Eleonora, there is nothing left but the Iron Phallus, Adams' nine-foot pistons.

4. ZOSSIMA'S CORPSE

We think we are clean, but are we? What does the Holy
Wormless Man beget but the horrible Worm, man? After
a long denial of the memory and the flesh of man we
assume that we have returned to him. However, when
Lazarus comes forth from the grave his raiment is not
morning sun and fresh-cut grass but damp scum and
mold. Today, the modern novelist, announcing a realistic
physical man, has spawned a fetal thing whose brains
and bones cause us, as Gulliver did, to put rue into our
nostrils. We are, finally, so defiled that we have to shriek

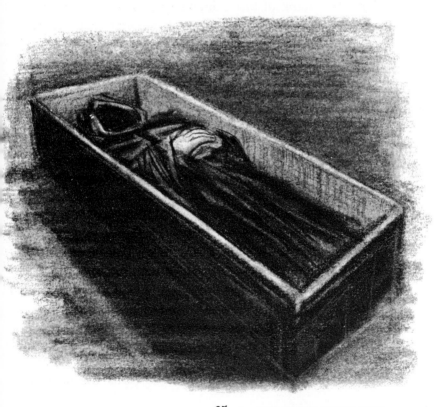

at the Uncleanness of our organs and functions in a cloacal, naturalistic literature. It was inevitable that we should become soiled. No other people in the world so needed to acknowledge their own odors, sweat and bowels as the American; so needed to know what the simplest dirty muzhik knows and accepts when he embraces and smells another peasant.

When you deny the male and female as they are, eating, sexually throbbing and giving off dense physical emanations, then you have the great STINK. Our misanthropy comes from one thing only, not man's poverty, politics, government, but the revulsion from his own ordure. As a result of this ablutionary ethic we produced a white and holy literature. But all holiness ends, as in *The Brothers Karamazov*, in the unspeakable stench of the corpse of Father Zossima. And so we, like those impiously cursing monks, are scurrying about and crying that, after all, the holiest men on earth smell, and despite Hawthorne, Thoreau and Poe, we still smell; thank heaven that we do; for if we did not we could not taste or touch or love or ache!

Today, we assume, we have a new naturalism in America. But all the masters, Shakespeare, Cervantes, Ben Jonson and the Poets of the Old Testament, gave us the sensual and naked man. We, however, are a self-educated people, always discovering new truths that were known several thousand years ago. Our own brand-new Whitman sang the Adamic Song of the Natural Man, he of the delicate bowels and the amorous wet. But Whitman's hymn to man is the very opposite of the naturalist's nausea. To the naturalist man is an accursed and evil smell; he peers into the subterranean pores, valves and orifices of the hair, the nails, the teeth, the mouth, looking for the satanic and sybaritic malodor. The naturalistic novel is the allegory of human ordure.

The cardinal sin against the Holy Ghost is not, as we know from Job and Whitman, to slaughter man, but to pillage and rob him of the cherished moistened kernel of his tissue and bones. No wonder Jonathan Swift moaned, "I will die on top first!" Nietzsche and Rimbaud had died a thousand times when they lived, but Dean Swift just decomposed. Job, who sat upon his dunghill, never lost the integrity that caused man to linger in his nostrils as milk and curd, but the Dean who wallowed in the molehills of the Lilliputs and in the huge offal of the Brobdingnags, could not revile noisome man enough. Swift was so tortured by his defecatory loathings that he had to reduce man to the meanest wight-like proportions so that Gulliver, by comparison, could be the massive excrement that man was to him. Pursued by his own hapless imaginings, he gave horrific girth and stature to the Brobdingnags so that he could paint in SIZE the vileness of the teeth, the nipples, the sickening unsightliness of eating, voiding and copulating. Could anything more horribly project his retchings than the battle between Gulliver and the enormous rats, those scavenger grave rats that forever prey upon the brain dying unto itself!

We have inherited Gulliver's malady. Out of the Brobdingnags and the Yahoos have come forth *McTeague, Vandover and the Brute*, and the Neanderthal Pleb of Proletarian muckraking literature. Swift's Gulliver is an inhuman groan; in some darkling covert of his tortured brain there is the prayer that man were not a defecating, eating and copulating animal; but in the spiteful nausea of Frank Norris there is nothing but matter in motion loathing itself.

What remains of man after we have read *McTeague*?—the beggarly memory of the gloomy dental parlor on Polk Street and McTeague stupidly making "mats" and plaster of Paris molds. McTeague has one desire, to purchase a huge Brobdingnagian gilded molar which he can hang out of the window facing Polk Street. A life-sized molar—that is his totem, his altar, his candled mass—something that has been extracted and spewed out of the mouth, an American golden MOLAR, a gaudy phallus.

That AMERICAN MOLAR stands between Aphrodite and ordure. The delicate monster, McTeague, cannot embrace the young and fragrant Trianna Sieppe because somewhere in the prognathous husk of his brain he sees her as an unsightly excreting female!

Job's dung heap and Whitman's *Leaves* are vindications of man's fragrant bowels, perspiration and skin. The great blasphemy in the Book of Job is committed in Satan's nostrils, in the attempt to pollute the odor of Job's flesh and to hide an alchemic ratsbane in his most secret mortal juices.

But Job's triumph over Satan lies not in his scriptural virtues or will, but in the remembrance of man's bones as sweet milk and curds. Job can scrape the boils from his body with a potsherd and still make an epithalamium for man: "His breasts are full of milk, and his bones are moistened with marrow."

And so Job returns to his flocks and vintage and lies with his wife, leaving behind him a memory of myrrh and balsam because the ingredients of man's aches, sorrows and flesh were always precious and goodly smelling to his nose and heart.

The soldiers of Gideon kneel down to drink from the springs of Circumstance with or without their spears and so they either go out to be warriors or are sent home to be the patient drudges of defeats or conquests in which they have had no part. Mistake not the legends of bondage: man contends with his gods to whom he is bondsman; Jacob wrestles for Light! and Job has more will and energy than Satan. Without that thrust against death and awful rot, we are misshapen. Does not the ghost of Hamlet's father go out to repair the injuries done to the blossom of his own life? The tears of Odysseus move us, because, homeless for twenty years, he never ceases to supplicate his nature: "Endure, my heart . . . endure," he cries until he reaches shore-dug Ithaca and Penelope. Doomed Saul consults the witch, the occult forces in Nature's cauldron, to augur for him. Yet he hurls his spear three times at his foreordained successor David. Macbeth murders not alone for power and lust, but as tragical heroes must, to avoid what seems predetermined. Saul *is* slain in battle and Macbeth *does* fall when the Woods of Birnam move, but they make the soothsayers, the Weird Sisters, the darksome atoms, prove themselves. Betwixt man's unsolved limits and nature's mandates lie the five acts of tragedy; and he who refuses to make these assaults upon the unknown denies himself some unguessed dimension. When Dostoevski's government clerk says, "I am sorry for life," does not the Universe itself pause to sigh forth its pang of pain and so burst a thread in its own destiny. Does not that dark and superstitious artist soul, Dostoevski, hope and tremble for such a cataclysmic incident.

The touchstone of the "ratiocinative" novel is mimicry, and not utterance. The American writer does not express the world, but copies it and lets it sieve through him.

There is no more dismal misconception of creation, or de-energizing act, than this sieving of the times.

The Greek word mimesis does not mean imitation; the mime or actor who put on a mask, the "skin of a beast or the feathers of a bird," as Jane Harrison writes in *Ancient Art and Ritual*, did not do so "to copy something or someone who is not himself, but to emphasize, enlarge, enhance, his own personality . . . he masquerades, he does not mimic." From the craft of Mark Twain to the ventriloquistic devices of Sinclair Lewis, as in *Babbitt*, the American writer has been a mimic of his period. He has not enlarged but diminished himself in order to represent his times.

The protomale is the very opposite of Dostoevski's clerk; doomed by rank, enslaved by poverty, he has pains, moods and tears as large and convulsive as Achilles'.

Today we have no patience with "unrecognizable" characterizations, with an unforeseen reaction or impulse, that appears to be out of the orbit of the person who has been fixed. How we abuse Herman Melville because Ahab is perchance a monologue and not REAL. We forget what totally unpredictable men and women the tragical heroes and heroines of Shakespeare are. How often they step out of their dramatic frames and talk those amazingly prophetic but dislocated lines—how the cuckold Troilus speaks, not out of himself, but from the abysses of the cracked heart of the Saint of all literature.

There is no more tedious credo than the realism of the behavioristic novel. We contemplate with devout wonder the HAND of Rembrandt in the *Self-Portrait*. The HAND, the fatted ruin of the flesh, cannot be doubted, nor can the pitiless struggle against mean decay be mistrusted; but as we look at the fingers, the knuckles, the nails, so

dimensionally faultless, we see IDEAL ANATOMY. The HAND
is the palpitating mask of an IDEA. Rembrandt's HAND is a
concrete, fleshly human limb, and also an IDEAL, just as the
barber's basin is to Sancho Panza what it optically repre-
sents as well as the HELMET OF MAMBRINO.

6. THE PROLETARIAN EUCHARIST

In the proletarian authors the black yeast of guilt is mixed
with the eucharistic body of the suffering masses; in Jack
London and Norris the pariah shame and miseries become
the plaguy afflictions of a class. London's carnivorous lust
is transmuted into socialist teachings. In him naturalism
and revulsion are one cankered, miserable skin. In Erskine
Caldwell's proletarian novels his satanic malady is meta-

morphosed into a moral precept, a yea-saying communistic rite. What was before a diabolical ecstasy for corpses is translated into a fervor for the poor untouchables. In his necrophagous novels the bitter corpse-lust becomes the dismembered cadaver of the stricken masses; the "converted" author can now at will dissever a head, a finger, a leg; for instead of the comedy of a picaresque brutality in which the leg or foot is buried in a lard pail behind a woodshed, it is the worker's body that is mutilated in a remorseless Class Struggle. It is the same in the fiction of Dos Passos and James T. Farrell, in which rapine and abortions are wantonly divulged as the degradation of the toiling workman. The proletarian populace is the ritual bull that must be killed and eaten so that society, the corpse of the masses, can be reborn!

What tartuffery there is in a literature for the PEOPLE. In the savioristic novels of proletarian rebirth, nothing is revivified. Expurgate the "stolen" Marxian vocabulary of one hundred words or less, and the remaining husk of pleb consciousness is the same as in the decadents. Witness the dialectical withering away of man in the capitalistic lazar-house, and participate in his seeming purgation through the mystery of the Mythic Strike. The stage is set for a proletarian Faustian drama, but across it stalks not Tamerlaine but Mickey Mouse—the "Colossus of the little," as Wyndham Lewis describes the contemporary protagonist.

The Strike fails as tragic purification, as a psychic ablution; the strike is barter, a pragmatic expedient, not a way of seeing. As a mythic source, as image or sacrament, it is much less than the mass or eucharistic monstrance. The drama of Bread can never be a substitute for the Wine and the Wafer, because man must not only have his loaf of bread, but he must also have an image to eat. Communism and fascism fail as awe and wonder. They are weak as image-making sources. And where there is a penury of mystery, superstition and wonder, terror is sure to follow. Man must appease his appetites. He will drink Christ's blood, or his beloved's, or she his. When his nature cannot find surcease in the dismemberment of Osiris, Christ or the ritualistic bull, it will seek it through "sacrificial" bloodshed; here is the meaning of all the ideologies. Give man some mead for his sybaritic senses; let him feed upon icons, if he be a lower slavish nature, or, if a higher, gentler one, upon poems, music, paintings, words, sounds, meadows and mountains. The great poems of slaughter and horror, like Marlowe's *Tamburlaine* or Goya's Saturn eating his son, not only make man's man-eating nature known to him, and so purify and appall him, but they also gratify his nethermost lusts. When a race, or a people, cannot be transmuted into visionaries, seers or strong iconoclastic spirits, they must then have their superstitions. Man cannot be denied the IMAGE.

Sociologic, proletarian literature is almost imageless; there are no stars, nights or dawns, no nature to touch, soften or ennoble man. He has no heroic orbit in which to wander and talk. He slinks along mean, swart streets, burrows through coal holes and nasty furnished rooms. Man is no large comment upon life, but just a rank, tumorous outgrowth of it. Are not poverty and ugliness just as "real" in the Russian novel? Look at a Chekhov hero; give him a wisp-like fragrance from an acacia blossom, a skein of lilac sky, and he loves the more the woman who has rejected him or the superior who has insulted him. Those who have tread upon him he includes; for he can sup upon his wounds and feed his senses and brains. Take Dostoevski's clerk: when he says that he is more ashamed of his poverty than anything else, and that he hides it like a thief who is afraid of being found out, he declares, ". . . I am as vain as though I had been skinned and the very air blowing on me hurt." He shames life, society and men more for having put this shabby coat and existence around him than all the calculated hardships and miseries of the proletarian novels which are tables of simple addition.

Gorki's tramps, the nomadic Chelkash so powerfully drawn out of the leafless earth of Russia, have huge, twisted agonies; thwarted and oppressed, they are finally their own fates; the furies in them can meet and kindle and sometimes extinguish the FURIES of the world. They wander over the barren, gnarled land, their hopes encumbered and sorrowfully defeated. Poverty limits and defines their lives and horizons, but does not altogether debauch their spirits. A man in Russian literature, be he so impoverished or balked, walks like a proverb.

7. MELANCHTHA

The American is underground and he cries for blood, for place, even for ordure, because it is human and will give him back the earth wisdom and knowledge of what man was.

This clamor for blood, for human offal, is a cry for dim and fetal beginnings. What do the behavioristic embryos in William Faulkner and Ernest Hemingway signify? The idiots and children in Faulkner's novels are symptoms of race amnesia.

In Faulkner's novels all life processes are reversed—rotting wood, puling skies, moist and bony moonbeams ache and pour forth life's pulse, while human consciousness just scantly exists. The wet rainy shadows and the muddied smelly leaves are anthropomorphically animate —"twilight ran in like a quiet violet dog," "rain-perplexed tears," "bearded watching trees." But the characters are denatured—Talliaferro in *Mosquitoes* has a "desiccated look, like a recently extracted tooth"; Jenny has "soft wormlike fingers"; Cecily Saunders, an "epicene unemphatic chin," "sexless knees" and "boneless hands." After such an immersion the reader himself is inoculated, like Sophia, who, Heine said, got consumption from reading Novalis's *Heinrich von Offendingen.*

The child-cult, animism, anthropomorphism and primitivism, pass over into manic cruelty and murder. Faulkner mutilates his men and women; he reduces them to embryonic size, cretin width, as Popeye, in *Sanctuary,* who decimates kittens and ravishes Temple Drake with a corncob. Time in the Faulkner novel is macerated; man is rifled of his potency and speech; his language is the "nails in the wound" of the WORD.

The anti-hero apostrophizes not the northern lights, but the latrine. Faulkner's Januarius Jones contemplates his beloved with "yellow eyes" that wash over her "warm and clear as urine." Says another Faulkner character, "I am Julian Lowe, I eat, I digest, I evacuate." The American does not journey to Hippocrene, but to the African Bushman to attend the scatological wedding feast of Melanchtha and the new god Feces. The modern American novel is like the hymeneal apparel of a Hottentot which Lessing describes: "Her arms and legs were entwined with the shining entrails of an heifer; from her neck there hung a pouch composed of the stomach of a kid."

The fetal hero is Hemingway's too: here the massacre of brain, speech and reason is a sacrament. He is a swinger of gore-censers, and a literary Caligula. Hemingway can break the slim, flowing neck of a kudu in a firm thrusting sentence, or perform a Caesarian operation with a jack-knife in a remorseless phrase. Violence induces in him a dreamy rhapsodical tenderness and he will pause, just before the orgiastic spell, to describe an aureole of spring rain falling upon the heads of six cabinet ministers about to be executed, or caressingly linger to paint the ecstatic and willowy quiver of a dying deer or limn the throbbing Goya-like flesh wound of a gored horse.

Doubt, sorrow and thought he cannot apprehend or scent; when he is reflective, he acquires the speech impediment of Melanchtha. What does it all come to in Hemingway and Faulkner, Dos Passos and Caldwell, London and Norris? The whole human fabric has collapsed, and man has fallen from the grace of good and evil into ordure. Remorse has been superseded by the kidneys, the prostate gland and the intestinal tract. The old

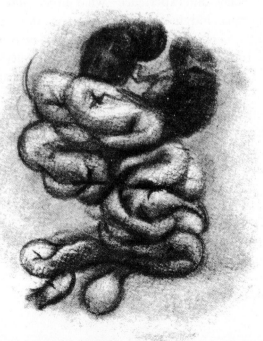

masters are no more, the eternal tragedies are concluded. The noble problems of man, love, anguish, evil and death, are done—aye, Madame Bovary and Manon Lescaut, the Camellias and Consumption, have had to give way to the realism of sublunary decaying Matter, to sputum, to vomiting spells, and to *The Sun Also Rises*.

In the Puritan Christian cosmogony spirit was not rooted in flesh, just as now matter performs and behaves as though mind were not of it. The demented dervish of MATTER goes on without a past, a tradition or a memory.

8. EZEKIEL'S VALLEY

The refusal of memory has given us a religion of place. American literary criticism has become a quest for memorial landmarks. Chant aloud the streets, cities, rivers— Locust, Cherry, Walnut, Topeka, Kansas City, the Missouri River—and you have American Literature. Our ritual of names belies our experience: what ironic and embittered chagrins, hid in the charred heart, are cast up, as nostalgic mementos, in the sacral names of American towns. Nature, when impeded, mocks man into crying out his desires. In *Life on the Mississippi* those scavenger river towns, afar from the orchards, temples and Pharaoh's sphinxes, were christened Little Egypt, Thebes, Memphis and Cairo! Finally, those abortive mud settlements, built as dirty Golcondas of gain, were washed away by the Mississippi River that had been called CONCEPTION by the priest Marquette. What sardonic defeats are in those defaced towns, Napoleon, Hard Times! We canonize our most barren and villainous penury; Carson City, Gopher City, Milk River, Huck Finn's castaway and tatterdemalion Missouri towns, those flowerless, alkali Eldorados, have become literary, metaphysical cartography. Our most craven fetish is nostalgia, which is always a stumbling block to perception. We garner the rivers, levees and towns with the piety of one telling the beads of a rosary. From *A Week on the Concord and the Merrimac* through *Huckleberry Finn* and *Winesburg, Ohio,* our literature is conceived as a eucharistic sacrament of American Geography. That lovely apocryphal place, in *Winesburg, Ohio,* of spirit and flesh, pollinated with sun-lit pining, sexual aches and orchard desires, is located for the reader by the insertion of a map that dots the site of the Water Works Pond! Names and places, nothing more, are the holy sepulcher of the dust, earth and stone in our Cave of Macphelah, and by their remains, we say, we belong here. But do we?

The commemoration of locality is the rationale of American novels and paintings: look at our canvases, at the embalming of a Chippendale chair, a gas lamp, the small town dry goods store in Speicher or Burchfield: Speicher's flesh has a *locale* wax, a *period* hue. Take the national Chaplin mime; he is a nostalgic daguerreotype. The American laughs and weeps over him as over a past and deceased locality—a dated Bowery still, a piece of 1905 sidewalk, a stereopticon of a saloon. We claim a poet or a novelist, when he is home-sown, of Arkansas mud-flats, Nebraska corn or St. Louis levees. Mark Twain's own homesickness was to be somewhere, to define his identity in a past, to contain himself wholly in pinchbeck memorabilia of the U.S.A., and not TO BE.

The mimic substitutes size, time and place for consciousness. Lacking the intuitive dimension, the mimic *paints* things and people instead of uttering them. He is the conventional outside artist who gives us the most "realistic" clothes, streets, dialects. He paints, adding to what is not deeply imaged upon his brain. In literature the parts are never equal to the whole. Whitman put together, piecemeal, his cosmos of goods, materials and joys, just as Twain added up the bits and surfaces of the Mississippi into a logarithm table. Lessing writes in *Laocoön* that Homer did not "paint" his characters; the beauty of Helen is known to the reader solely by the eyes of the old men as they approach her.

The artist who cravenly submits to time, place and space confesses his own limits. The oracles knew not time; the poet's testament is the oath of the Angel in the Apocalypse that there will be no more time. The moment in which Mahomet gazes upon "all the habitations of Allah" is not long enough for the water to be spilt from the pitcher. Christ walks upon water in a visionary sea; Myshkin, in *The Idiot*, has his ecstatic premonition of infinity when he has an epileptic fit. We know the inward size of an artist by his dimensional thirsts, the gigantic windmills of Don Quixote.

Know true literature by its dimensional signature. Melville's tragedy is Puritanic and Elizabethan. Melville's tempests have the wrath, blood and measure of a Faustian universe. Hamlet, Macbeth, Prospero and Myshkin are rapturous idiots, dying out of the dimensional world. Macbeth dwells in a Cave of Terror, upon which are shadowed the eternal Forms; and Prospero lives in his apocryphal and visionary isle with an Ariel, a sprite that has dominion over all matter. The spatial appetites of man are limitless. Man's brain is the globe upon which the terrains and melancholy meads of brit cast their evening shadows. The pursuit of evil—the ontological White Whale—is Dionysiac, but the hero, Ahab, is a cloven-footed Puritan gargoyle.

Locality and consciousness have never co-existed in the American novel. In Twain the Mississippi becomes the Sanctuary of Place, "the body of the nation." Compare the anatomy of Twain's Mississippi with Melville's Orphic measurements of the Whale in the cetology chapter.

We have laid Being in a small plot of ground called American Place to sob with the fanged worms. Listen to Edgar Poe: "The consciousness of *being* had grown hourly more indistinct, and that of mere *locality* had usurped its position. The idea of entity was becoming merged into that of *place*. The narrow space immediately surrounding what had been the body, was now growing to be the body itself."

The breach between Don Quixote and Gulliver is as wide as the cleavage between Melville, Emily Dickinson

and Poe, artists of memory, and the rural folk bards, Mark Twain and Sherwood Anderson. There are two genres of literary culture in America, the reflective poetry of memory and the mimic folk art.

The rural poet chants the peasant psalmodies of birth, habit, work, marriage and coition, again and again in the same mood and cadence. His is the raw pioneer hymn of average people, of homely, "private" reminiscence, and not the larger lore and vision of man's past. He sings until he grows weary, old or mute—until time drains him of the honey in his veins. This is the cycle of Sherwood Anderson, Twain-mimic and folk-poet.

The one refrain in Anderson's books, in *Winesburg, Ohio, Triumph of the Egg,* and *Many Marriages* is Return, Return, O Shulamite, just as Dreiser, forever the Preacher in Ecclesiastes, always laments the futility of the grieving flesh: "Vanity of vanities, all is vanity." Anderson and Dreiser never get much beyond the agitations of the genital organs: man throbs and breeds, but does not think, knows not the Gehenna of metaphysical laceration. In Dreiser the flesh broods on its chemic corrosion and stands inexplicable before cosmic evil—finally to utter, what?— "endless space and unutterable loneliness." "Oh, endless order. Oh, endless disorder! Death without life! Life without Death!"

It is no accident that the most carnal poem, The Song of Songs, and the psalm of satiety and weariness, Ecclesiastes, are among the briefest in the Old Testament. There are planetary reaches and saturnine chasms in man unknown to the hedonist and the naturalistic Preacher of Pity. Spikenard, cypress and the myrrh of Lebanon dilate the nostrils and free the aching pores: sated, the Epicure sheds tears but has no ashy, cindery grief. The voluptuaries of the carnal body and the decaying flesh neither make "the sparks fly upward" to bind the Pleiades nor descend into the cracked and clinkered Hades of the Heart.

However, no poet has so breathed "the fragrance of myself," the "scented herbage" of hands, hair, mouth and organs, male and female, as Sherwood Anderson. "Who goes there," called Walt Whitman, "hankering, gross, mystical, nude," and one man in America has the right to answer, "I, Sherwood Anderson, walk, speak and breathe, so!"

Anderson is not so grandiose; he does not stalk Manhatta, the grassy, bedewed midlands of Ohio and Wisconsin as vigorously as Whitman; but he is a more exquisite singer. You can sup upon the Edenic mead of Anderson's herbivorous and cow-scented words, graze and low upon the soft-humped pasture lands of his hay-tufted sentences.

Anderson's artless tales, warm meadowy pollen blown from the Garden of Genesis, recall the Russian poet who wrote:

> I know not myself what I will sing,
> But only my song is ripening.

Poor White, Winesburg, Ohio and *Many Marriages* are no apotheoses of an embalmed and *dated* period. They are auguries of the drought that would turn America into Ezekiel's Valley of Dry Bones. A blighted, but not hopeless agrarian land of farmhouses, handiwork and leafy evenings was about to be mired upon and debauched. Whatever frugality these rural Americans had had, they had known no complete denial of fieldy smells, wood odors, streams, those lucent drops of nature that succor the fingers, the mouth and the organs, as deeply as food, sex, sleep and work.

The lonely city biped is denied flowers and hills; chained to the machine, celled in the mechanized room, inclosed in the theoretic sidewalk, he treads his vasty Asias and Indias upon a screen, gazing at dithering, husked heaths, travelogue terrains and Himalayas. Denied rondured vistas, he is given instead a bogus dimension, an interior which is added *on* to drained, splayed objects; cozened of pigments, his thirsts are slaked upon "Technicolor" reds, greens and ambers, which are spilled *on*. The automobile, the radio and the films are mechanical anesthesia-horrors which give man all the counterfeit moods of travel, sound, *acting*, vocal utterance, while insidiously depriving him of motion, energy, act, human speech and animate contact.

American History has been one long pillage and destruction of ideals, culture, cities and hamlets. The myth of progress has led us into the villainous definitions of man, art and city. It has taken us far underground, where we wander over flowerless and treeless plains of macadam, feeding upon the ruby leakages of neon lights.

American civilization is "deanimated," "metronomic," a grotesque enlargement of that "gap between touch and thing," as William Carlos Williams writes in "Jacataqua." The first commandment of the manic, machine age is, "Thou shalt not TOUCH." But deny man touch and the Human Hand becomes impotent. This is the fable and portent of *Winesburg, Ohio*.

The artisan and lover are one. Useful hands have the same winged subtleties when they caress a woman's body, lips and hair. Take these away and the inshut, sullen hands "strike"; they break forth into furied bacchanals. "Befoul the workmen's tools and materials long enough," says Gilbert Cannan, whom Anderson quotes in *Winesburg, Ohio,* "and in the end the workmen will turn on you and kill you."

In *Many Marriages* Anderson cannot announce love without feeling that he is a little demented. He writes: "If one seek love and go towards it directly as one may in the midst of the perplexities of modern life, one is perhaps insane." There is in Anderson a dark misgiving that the birthright of man and woman has been stolen, and that the fingers and the body have lost their wisdom, uses and memory. The artist is forever longing for the hills and valleys of Judea, the primal instincts. Somewhere in Sherwood Anderson's mind is a vague and forlorn belief that men and women have forgotten how to lie with one an-

other. For the modern, "scientific" man and woman are halves, before, during, and after the sexual sacrament. The lonely male biped spills his seed as perilously as Onan did.

Anderson returns to the Bible so that he may not become insanely American. The pining artist begins *Many Marriages* in the simple organ accent of Job:

> There was a man named Webster lived in a town of twenty thousand people in the State of Wisconsin.
>
> There was a man in the land of Uz, whose name was Job.

He conjures up Genesis, the Song of Songs: he repeats memorized cadences out of the Old Testament to recall unto himself how man once entered woman. The whole of *Many Marriages* is a mnemonic and erotical variation on: "and he went in unto Hagar, and she conceived."

John Webster, in *Many Marriages*, desires to pull down all the erotical walls of Jericho. The images of woman's body upon his brain smell of spikenard, myrrh and the garments of Lebanon. Faulkner, once a disciple of Anderson, dismembers man in his purgatorial descent into the blood to revivify speech and memory. Sherwood Anderson simply undresses him: "When he was quite nude he got out the little picture of the Virgin and set it upon a kind of dresser that stood in a corner between the two windows. On the dresser he also placed the two candlesticks with the Christ on the cross on them and putting two of the yellow candles in them lighted the candles."

But this John Webster is a lunatic figure to his own creator. "Perhaps I am insane," the wavering Anderson permits Webster to say at the conclusion of *Many Marriages*. In the end both Anderson and Dreiser have taken the American way. Sherwood Anderson once said that the Americans are the most lonely people in the world. They are also the most fearful of their solitude. *Walden* and *Winesburg, Ohio* are fables of lonely grotesques living out their lives against the American Grain. Thoreau fled to Walden Pond and became one of the great cranks. Anderson, however, after his "flight" to *Winesburg, Ohio* and into *Many Marriages*, returned to Gath. Does not Anderson confess in both of those testaments that he did not dare to become an eccentric?

At the time of writing *Winesburg, Ohio*, Sherwood Anderson was one of the small rebel procession of odd and droll figures in America. We have Alfred Stieglitz's photograph of this bizarre child of the arts—the rural midland poet with fanatic eyes, the uncut hair bangs, the seedy, farmland visionary. He was a grotesque! "The moment one of the people took one of the truths to himself," wrote Anderson in *Winesburg*, "called it his truth, and tried to live his life by it, he became a grotesque and the truth he embraced became a falsehood." Beware of the poet who fears lying; for out of the leaven of such falsehood were kneaded *Walden, Leaves of Grass, Winesburg, Ohio*.

Winesburg, Ohio is the imaginary hermitage of all the bizarre people without whose cheating dreams, aerial thefts and intangible larcenies, America would have long since been doomed. Ye juiceless Philistines, what would have become of these Cash Register States without the cranks, the eccentrics, without the Oneidans, Brook Farmers, free lovers, anarchists and Bible communists? The cult, alas, and may the Furies be blessed, has saved America from total blight. Our whole culture is one half cult and one half humbug. It is in the parable of things and people, American, that Whitman, the divine mounte-

V

THE BRIDEGROOM'S ACHE

1. THE SINK OF BETHESDA

Jesus the bridegroom has perished; but the dogma, the ambiguous statutes, have endured: the nails, the cross, the hyssop, the dirty paraphernalia of sorrow, horror and belief have remained. The cup that was too galled for Christ—"Father, if Thou be willing, remove this cup from me"—has been drained by sectaries, visionaries, artists. A whole generation of poets, Emily Dickinson, Herman Melville, Thoreau, Poe and Whitman, went to Bethesda and to skulled Golgotha.

Melville traveled to the Holy Land for surcease and grace, to tarry at the sepulcher, at Bethesda, to gaze at Kedron's flow; but stayed to repine at the scrofulous Calvary relics, the cross-mongers, "Cloaca of remotest day." Melville found an impious, lousy Gethsemane.

Emily Dickinson sang with the crucifix Nails pressed upon her throat; the sybil of snowdrops and crocuses, who had quaffed God from "tumblers of clover," became the frugal evangel:

> Eternity, I'm coming, Sir, . . .
> A prayer is the little implement. . . .
> Promise this, when you be dying. . . .

It is idle doctrine to argue that a Poet could be less or more—to contend that the Blood could have spoken deeper abysses. No mortal is, or can be, more than he was: "And which of you by taking thought can add one cubit unto his stature?" Circe translates the drunken sailors of Odysseus into swine but does not alter them.

Christianity slowed the flame, the beat, the stuff of Personality. Whatever the American Poet uttered in bravery expired soon in denials, in gorged weariness, in Emily Dickinson's "In vision and in veto," or "Corinthian's bugle obliterates the birds."

How the Christian moan of ennui hovers over the Puritan; Emily Dickinson "plaited the residue of woe with monotony," and Thoreau bequeathed a bog as the Temple and the Table.

Yet we trumpet Emily Dickinson's straitened craft. Infolded Puritan lips become the beauteous, skeletal, Lacedaemonian line! And Emily Dickinson's apocalyptic poetry accents Christ's admonitory "Yea, yea; Nay, nay"; it is as life and vision, as we have observed it in the lowly and surly habits of Rappites, Shakers and Quakers, a jeopardy and chastisement.

And Thoreau's bog is what? the marsh, rocks, cindered veins of ravines, the charred and livid shells of trees lit by Charon's eyes. Nothing blooms here: all is doomed: "Dead Water Mountain," "dead water of Second Lake," of "Large Lake"; "Among the rivers which empty into the Merrimac, the Concord is known . . . as a dead stream."

Is this the serpent, or the fish?

All of Nature's Table is not for man, who sometimes has for repast Banquo's ghost.

There are many Natures—marsh, fen, mountain, mouse, bird, dove and men, whose touch, sight and smell yield a sweet Elysium or a reechy, blasted Erebus.

In Leviticus man is enjoined to keep the blood, the flesh and the brain, the altar of memory, undefiled. There are abominations in nature, fitch, kite, raven, rat or toad, that paint their loathsome image upon the tender mind: the body or raiment touched and fouled by these must be bathed; the earthen vessel upon which an Unclean Animal has fallen must be broken so that the veins may not unravel in revulsion. Had not Thoreau said that the Imagination is wounded long before the conscience, and then turned his own Pegasus into a reptile.

His star was blighted by the First Shame; he wrote, "our very life is our disgrace." Thoreau, like Adam after the Fall, hid in quagmire, mud and fen. How can fallen "man ascend pure and fragrant"? asked he who went INTO NATURE to be clean. His life was a sorcerer's mixing of separate natures. It was a devil's nuptial of man and pond, bird, pine, muskrat and ravine; "I fell in love with a scrub oak," "I felt a positive yearning toward one bush."

Thoreau's life is a half parable: to be PURE he cast out the devils, but entered the swine. His Nature is Bethesda's Sink in whose mired waters he sought ablution from the Fall.

Human literature and lore are a warm, loose bounty of the tongue—how tall Ulysses was when he sat, or how high Agamemnon was when standing. What noble gossip are Sancho's gristled proverbs. Here are the flour, grain, wine and barley, all the goodly, brewing curd and milk of talk. This is the BREAD for which we ask our Poets only to get a Stone—Thoreau's swamp, Emily Dickinson's burial sod, and Melville's watery grave.

2. THE FALSE ASCENSION

The nineteenth century socialist settlements, Economy, New Harmony, New Lebanon, Fruitlands, Oneida, and the visions of the poets, Thoreau's *Walden*, Emily Dickinson's poems, Poe's "Eureka" and Melville's *Billy Budd*, are New Testament allegories.

Celibate Thoreau, spinster Emily Dickinson, and the ascetic Shakers partake of the bread of original sin. Emily Dickinson, "Bride of the Holy Ghost," is garbed in white, the Shaker "wedding garment"; Moby Dick is clad in priestly levitical purity. The materials of American vistas, poems and communities, are the same. Pilgrim, Quaker, poet, or citizen were "mankind extinct in seraphim."

It was in the orchards of America that they made the communistic cradles of Golgotha. There was George Rapp, pietistic communist and Moravian vinedresser, and his grim god-throbbing band at Economy. They built fifty log cabins, a church, saw mill and tannery; preached continence, temperance and work, and taught "the dual nature of Adam" before the Edenic rib had been loosed.

Shaker mother Ann Lee, of quaint illiterate brain, enjoined communism, sparse speech, and angelical bachelordom, in pious and homely Matthew's vein: "For in the resurrection they neither marry." These American Essenes tenanted New Lebanon, tilled fields, built chairs, sold garden seed, apple sauce, floor mops and SHOOK!

Bronson Alcott, ascetic, teetotaler, Pythagorean law giver at Fruitlands, prohibited the eating of meat and forbade use of manure for soil. Like Thoreau, Alcott tried to banish man's brutish appetites, whatever was coarse and concupiscent. Thoreau went to the vestal calyx and the skunk cabbage to be released from carnal savors; Alcott prescribed meals of aerated, melodic fruits and vegetables that would fragrantly fumigate the intellect and exorcise sensual images. "The repugnance to animal food is not the effect of experience," said Thoreau, "but an instinct."

Alcott's regimen and Thoreau's disgust made havoc of the immutable human processes. Had not Moses, who tenderly cherished all the purities that elevate habit, said that Life, the SEED, is always clean;—whatever may "fall upon any sowing seed, which is to be sown, it shall be clean."

Upon the moan of denial and repulsion were community allegories conceived: "If thy hand offend thee, cut it off! If thy eye offend thee, pluck it out!" Of this was deep but doomed *Walden* made.

Their vision was a dying out of life. Espousing a sepulcher, they maimed their tongues and quelled their organs, and deemed them Risen! By edict, curtailment, by a rapt, remorseless plucking out of the human ache, they ascended!

Their faith was made up of humble, plain legends, the dingy miracles, the healings at Bethesda, the raising of Lazarus, the resurrection—the fable of three ignorant women who came with burial spices to the Tomb, and finding but a Linen Cloth, of it wove a Resurrection.

This is the False Ascension, call it *Walden*, or Shaker Utopia, or "Eureka." For neither Cup, nor Cross, nor Nails, nor Cloth, can yield a total vision and song; these can never bring man to Pisgah, or give him the trumpet for coveted Jericho. " 'Twas Christ's own personal expanse," uttered Emily Dickinson, "that bore him from the tomb."

Dogma and denial, Calvary or Nature, trampled the throat of poets and visionaries; doctrine doomed the flower, fruit and savor of their blood. How could they make the voice, the vined hair, and the flesh a Moab's harp, out of "If thy eye offend thee, pluck it out!"

Life brings its own thwarting, grief or light; nothing

can be foreknown; the deepest natures are mysterious unto themselves. Christ's Personality is the Ache that asked for a Kiss; Thoreau's is the Eye that shone upon snow, birch, leaf and sumac, without remotely dreaming or guessing the Light that it shed. All that man may know of good, evil, God, the earth or his own nature, is shadowed upon his organs, or on the walls of Plato's Cave. What can be ordained? Ask for a dream, an image, an intuition, will it be given? or a "dram of heaven," can it be had? The Cup, the Poem, the Light, are drunk in darkness, or else how could they be taken? Calvaries and Infernos are committed in the drained light on the Mount of Olives, or with the Shades.

Our poets, communal soothsayers, abjured the speech, hunger and blood, without which ideals and absolutes cannot be imagined. These star-garbed specters, who craved to plant an Elysium in the meadowy surf of the northern lights, were much less wise in love, conversation, habit and art than Goethe who said, "We ought to be and remain obscure to ourselves."

3. THE BRIDEGROOM

"To be human is more than to be divine, for when Christ was divine he was uncontented till he had been human."

EMILY DICKINSON

The Galilean dreamer unwittingly had bestowed a malign creed that had spawned anguished sects, and turned the songs of Melville, Emily Dickinson, Poe and Hawthorne into a vigil of the Tomb. Emily Dickinson had abjured the wasps, the bees, the broom and tulips and buccaneering bluebirds because "There is no trumpet like the tomb." And Herman Melville had renounced the Marquesan calabashes of fruits, oils, pomegranates, the doxologies of Leviathan, and the psalms of spermaceti and brit, to weep over "The Last prints of the Wounded Feet." He, who had gazed upon vernal sod of heaven and sea and looked in evening at the lunar jet of the White Bull, Jupiter, Leviathan, had shawled himself as Christly pilgrim, and espoused a haggard fast of silence. The artist, the sectary, as well as the tender, beclouded Jesus, had to assassinate his pulses to know Beatitude and Goodness.

Jesus no more understood his life, or his Text, than Emily Dickinson and Herman Melville comprehended their Christian art. There is in myth or history no more hapless enigma than Jesus, or Christian doctrine. The Teacher uttered contrary and wandering precepts, exhorting men to turn the other cheek, to love and honor parents, while also demanding, "If any man come to me, and hate not his father, and mother, and wife, and children, and brethren, and sisters, yea, and his own life also, he cannot be my disciple." He who denounced the flesh—"the flesh profiteth nothing"—made his own Body, the frail dreamer's skin, soothed and titillated by spikenard, dug and bled by nails, the Bread, the Image, the Altar. "He that eateth my flesh, and drinketh my blood, dwelleth in me, and I in him," he said, and dismayed his disciples. They murmured among themselves, "This is an hard saying: who can hear it?" The Jews asked, "How can this man give us his flesh to eat?" His little band was ready to desert him because he asked for the adoration and the kisses that have since been given to the dirty sacred relics, the hair, the bones, and the bloody wounds of the effigy in the church. Man, not to raven upon his own bones and the world's, must eat and drink the beloved Image or Person of a Francesca, Beatrice or Jesus.

No one more than Jesus could have been so easily betrayed by a kiss—for he, who knew *before* of the Treason, could not avert his face when "devil" Iscariot proffered his lips.

Jesus did not rebuke the Pharisee but entreated him when he said, "Thou gavest me no kiss: but this woman since the time I came in hath not ceased to kiss my feet." The Pharisee, having no "alabaster box of ointment" for Jesus, left his guest chagrined. Had not the house of Mary been filled with the odor of spikenard which she had put on his hair and feet!

His whole life was one entreaty: "See, I am a man." His ache for love was so constant that he frightened his disciples. He, himself, was abashed by the ache and beseeched his disciples who were ready to forsake him: "Doth this offend you" and "will ye go away?"

He could not make the twelve disciples understand that Christ, Man and Messiah, is Body. Poor Jesus, his own ghost in torment because the stupid flock refused to believe that he was flesh and bones, ate bread, broiled fish and honeycomb with them! "Behold my hands and feet," uttered the Holy Ghost, "that it is I myself: handle me and see!"

At the Last Supper Jesus disrobed himself to show that he was flesh. Here was the Revelation! Naked, he bowed down in jubilance before those whom he loved, and washed their feet. "If I wash thee not, thou hast no part with me."

"Ye call me Master and Lord: and ye say well; for so I am," spoke Jesus, the bridegroom. But all was in vain: the life, the acts, the Supper, the adoration of the feet. Peter

was shocked: "Thou shalt never wash my feet." "Know ye what I have done to you?" Jesus had asked, after he had put on his garment and sat at the table. They did not know.

Could men believe in one another there would be no sick, no blind, no poor; were not five thousand fed with five barley loaves and two fishes? Jesus would raise the dead for those who loved him.

What tender and enchanted soul has not said in his heart to the leper, "Be thou clean," and to the palsied, "Arise, and take up thy couch."

A man who believes he is the Son of God requires infinite faith. Like Francesca and Paolo, the lightest wind bore him to a compassionate glance. Indifference, skepticism and hostility, however, destroyed Jesus: Simon Peter, Thomas, and especially rebel Judas, troubled him. Had not quaint, little Thomas so disturbed Jesus that the Holy Ghost not only addressed himself first to the *Doubter*, but commanded him to fix the print of his nails into the Ghost's flesh to see whether it was not Christ!

With his faithful ones he was "Master and Lord"; when he was met, upon his entrance into Jerusalem, with hosannas and palm branches, his nature sang: "Behold, thy King cometh, sitting on an ass's colt." But before Pilate, Caiaphas and Herod, the State, he was abject. "Art thou the King of the Jews?" asked Pilate. "Thou sayest it," replied Jesus. "Art thou the Son of God?" demanded the elders and the chief priests. "Ye say that I am," responded Jesus. To Herod he answered nothing.

Jesus did not love all equally. Some men he despised; Judas Iscariot he hated. For all the disciples, save one, the Supper was a troth of love. For Iscariot it was a tribunal.

Here is the Supper: The disciples have eaten: Jesus has bathed their feet. To the eleven he has been a bridegroom; one, however, he judges. John is leaning upon the Master's breast as Jesus chastises Judas: "I say unto you that one of you shall betray me." "Woe unto that man by whom the Son of Man is betrayed."

Of the twelve none suffered so much as Judas Iscariot. Between Judas and Jesus there existed an enmity inflamed by wounds and venom. Judas, stung and pilfered of a disciple's love and faith, had spewed forth envy and spite, when Jesus in his glory had received from Mary's hand the pound of ointment for his feet: "Why was not this ointment sold for three hundred pence, and given to the poor?" Jesus, no less quick to smart, had replied: "For the poor always ye have with you; but me ye have not always."

Was despised Judas "thief," "devil" and "unclean"? Were he foreordained "Satan," did he not require pity more than all? Was he not then Nature's malice, not his own? Why did not Jesus turn the other cheek to Judas?

Is Judas as evil as Jesus thinks him? The disciples see him dimly and variously. Matthew paints a base and cynic kiss: "Hail, Master"; while Mark tells of a throbbing betrayal, "Master, Master."

To those who had come to take Jesus away, Iscariot had said: "Lead him away, safely." And, when he knew Christ's fate, the "thief" returned to the temple, cast down the silver before the priests, and condemning himself and their perfidy, spoke: "I have betrayed the innocent blood." From there he departed to hang himself.

The eleven had fled, leaving Jesus naked, to be covered with a piece of linen cloth by a compassionate stranger. Peter, swearing and cursing to save himself, had thrice denied Jesus: "I know not this man." Of the twelve, one alone, he of Kerioth, "Satan" Iscariot, had taken his life for the Master.

Did not Judas love Jesus? And did not Jesus deny Judas? He had given tender surnames to the disciples, but Judas he had named Traitor. At the Table Iscariot was the pariah witness of the embraces and wooing glances of Jesus and his beloved ones. But Jesus could not revile him enough: "Ye are not all clean." "One of you is a devil." Jesus smote him—"That thou doest, do quickly"—until he thrust him out. Then, when he had sent away him whom he had CHOSEN to betray him, his heart rejoiced: "Now the Son of Man is glorified."

Did Judas betray Jesus for thirty pieces of silver? Nay. For a Kiss Judas betrayed Jesus!

Peter, thrice denying his Christ, pays an easy, sufferable penance by sobbing out his remorse; whilst Judas hangs himself, and proffers an unloved body for vulture's food.

What does the Teacher teach? Can wickedness, depravity, cunning and lust be changed? Tell a man not to resist evil with evil, will he do it? "Lord, how oft shall my brother sin against me, and I forgive him? Till seven times?" entreats Peter. When the soldiers, however, come to take Christ, Peter cuts off the ear of Malchus, Caiaphas's servant.

Will charity speak, when vanity must? Christ cannot turn the other cheek to Judas. Jesus had to be betrayed to stand revealed: neither Jesus, Judas nor Peter may be altered; love, venom, malice and anger emit their own pure scents. "Nothing can destroy the soul, not even its own wickedness," says Plato: nothing must.

Jesus' own edicts thwarted him; the Messiah who cried, "I come to bring fire and the sword," denied the lover

who beseeched the Pharisee for a kiss. The Rabbi, who
overthrew the tables of the money-changers and the seats
of the dove-venders, tarnished the man who bathed the
disciples' feet.

Jesus knew little of the covert appetites: the ruined
blood, the furnace veins, the cunning whoring logic of the
flesh. The carpenter's son had on occasion sat with some
publicans, winebibbers; had consorted with mendicants,
the poor and the humble; but like Whitman, he had only
one song, the Bridegroom's Ache: "Thou gavest me no
kiss: but this woman since the time I came in hath not
ceased to kiss my feet."

The Galilean, who in his heart had healed the sick, the blind, and cast out the devils of men, believed that everyone could sit down with Abraham, Isaac and Jacob upon Heaven's grassy hillocks. Man was good. Who could not love his enemies? Who would not cut off his offending right hand to save his soul? Was there a man who would give a serpent to him who asked for fish? Could not water be turned into wine and the whole of life be a marriage of Cana?

Moses, too, was a gentle dreamer, and more humble than Jesus; he was so meek that he would not utter laws unless the Lord put them into his mouth. The monotheist, the idol-breaker, could not be taskmaster to Pharaoh's suffering bondmen; when the children of Israel wept because they had been smitten by snakes, he made them a fiery serpent of brass, a homeopathic image, to cure them! The temple he designed for Jehovah, wrought of the aromatic odors of lebanon wood and of gold and brass, was a pagan memory of the molten image; and the statutes he gave he put into an Ark of carnal shittim wood. The laws he delivered were softly hinted and sung:

> My doctrine shall drop as the rain . . .
> the small rain upon the tender herbs.

His dietary injunctions were a supplication to the heart's delicacy; he tried to teach the heathen slaves pity: not to eat a kid seethed in its mother's milk, not to raven upon blood. And his sabbatical decrees for the toiling earth and the burdened beast were an invocation to human gentleness.

No prophet ever despised leadership more than Moses. He, who had been denied all, Canaan, the grape, the fat kidneys of wheat and the kine, he, whose soul, parched by manna and the wilderness, was a psalm to the flocks and fresh sweet waters—"Spring up, O well; sing ye unto it"—could not be harsh to these Children who had sobbed so bitterly for the cucumbers, the melons and the leeks of Egypt; and so he gave them a Sabbath, a rest, from all ordinances and prohibitions. "Thou mayest eat flesh, whatsoever thy soul lusteth after," Moses told them. Besides, what could he do if these savage little carnivores just had to eat kites, vultures and eagles!

Moses also had communal visions, but he knew the animal, Man. Although he apportioned, equally, food, manna and possessions, he announced that all debts were

to be revoked every seventh year! He also made a Jubilee of every fiftieth year in which all lands and houses were to be returned to their original owners!

This meek man, he alone whom God dared to face, he who died without leaving a sepulcher, was more of a worker and leader among people than Christ.

Jesus had a sweet temperament, spun like the lilies of the field which toil not: the pinings for the lover's spikenard, not the statutes and the denials, disclose his character.

Neither the holy tablets, nor the Sermon on the Mount, unravel Jahweh or Jesus; the hints of their whims, angers, loves are not here. Jahweh and Jesus dote upon David and Peter no less than the aged king of Israel fondles his vain and erring Absalom. Why was good, sad Saul or Judas denied grace? The sensual, olive-complexioned Player of the Harp may lust after Bathsheba, send her Hittite husband to battle to be killed, and yet live out his years with a virgin to warm his crabbed bones, until he is gathered unto his fathers, while Saul's fate seethes in a witch's pot, and Judas's end is hanging.

VI

THE CROSS AND THE WINDMILLS

Both Christ's and Don Quixote's folly are committed in a deep trance. The dread of Crucifixion—"My time is not yet come"—and Don Quixote's combat with the windmills, so like Verhaeren's "masts of dementia," are ecstasies. Christ and the Knight of the Sorrowful Countenance are under the spell of the "machina of follies"; they behave automatically, as Pascal said, out of the necessity to finish. All who pursue holy grails do so as clairvoyant automatons; they are suffering somnambulists: they walk on water, fight sheep and windmills, free Virgin Mary icons, and dwell in an opaque and aching concord with all impossibilities.

Living beyond probable limits, or pulsing for infinity, they invade a universe that is always receding; objects are ideally, or chivalrously, gorged to give destiny size. "Grief expands time," said Emily Dickinson. "He who increaseth wisdom increaseth sorrow," spoke the preacher in Ecclesiastes.

The man of sorrows lengthens time, space and the universe. Melville chose the Atlantic as the Cup of Gruel from which the Leviathan could feed. Don Quixote's race of giant windmills have arms "almost two leagues long." Sancho Panza is not less enchanted, for when Sancho, who has been in service but three months, asks Don Quixote for twenty years' wages, he is not so moved by craft, or materialistic inevitability, as by ideal delusion. Don

Quixote had not asked his squire in vain to see the windmills as giants.

All lose their reason, the Martyr, the Knight, and the Squire: the head-cudgelings that Don Quixote suffers cast him into a rapture, without which the sheep could not be armies nor the inns castles.

Don Quixote resolves to see whatever is common, rank or rude—a barber's basin, an Asturian wench, an inn —with chivalry. "Born to live dying," the Knight is saved from absolute Platonism and Christian asceticism by his squire, Sancho Panza. Sancho accepts his Master's tragedy, the enchantment and the madness; he grieves that inns, Poor Johns, whores and sheep are not castles, trout, ladies and armies; Sancho will look with enough optical valor and knight-errantry to swear that they are, and must be, if the Agony is to be borne; but he will not reject their necessary and natural forms.

Quixote's folly begins, not in a holy Bethlehem manger, but in the stable where the innkeeper reads the orison of knighthood out of a straw and barley ledgerbook. At the muleteer's cistern, where the Good Knight has set down the counterfeit beaver and the ridiculous armor, Don Quixote teaches subtle graces and courteous understanding by cracking the pates of any who dare defile these cudgels of vision. Mounted on dry, skinny Rosinante, he divulges his heart to the Divine Wench, the impalpable Dulcinea of Toboso, "who had the best hand of powdering porks of any woman in the Mancha," and rides away to fight rabble brains, friars, barbers, curates and carriers.

The Madness never becomes a piety. For Don Quixote, in his sacred quest of goodness and renunciation, is never without Sancho, who, astride his ass, accompanies his Lord and Spirit with wallet, food and bottle.

The Knight has two services to commit: one to recover courtesy in the world, and the other to assail the frocked virtues. Gentle speech, tender civilities there must be. Each rude encounter and base mischance hurls the Sweet Man of the Mancha, who would oppose the cormorant world with a pasteboard visor and an ideal understanding, into long fainting spells. Don Quixote's speech blows forth so dolorously, because some muleteer, or jackanapes, denies that even one knight errant yet lives upon the earth! "I would speak more mannerly, if I were such a one as thou art," rails Don Quixote, amazed that a common lout and officer can be so without fragrant breeding that he cannot perceive a humble believer of the Christian faith standing before him. "Is it the custom of this country, you bottle-head! to talk after so rude a manner to knight errant?" His charge to Sancho that he never engage in battle at his side save against the vulgar and the base is his supplication and trust that most men are civil and discerning.

Even of tradesmen the knight-errant expects human bounties. When the Merchants of Toledo demand coarse proof that his Madonna Dulcinea is that Beauty he declares her to be, Don Quixote, outraged and undeceived, challenges, ". . . proud, unreasonable folk," "If I did show her to you, what mastery were it then to you to acknowledge truth so notorious?"

The innkeeper may dupe and thwack him, and read his prayer of knighthood out of a varlet's register, yet Don Quixote will pardon him, certain that after malice, raillery and guile have had their natural vent, honesty and virtue will speak.

A Fool's ass's milk his heart jets. He elevates all mankind. The ugly trollop, Maritornes, he endows with hair of "the glisteringest gold of Arabia." Why can he not enchant the whole world and turn infidel carriers, clotpolls, Maritornes and the Merchants of Toledo, into believers? Goodness must announce itself. Is it not enough, when Don Quixote angrily admonishes the cruel farmer for whipping the boy Andrew, that Justice has spoken to Error? "Today did he take away the whip out of that pitiless enemy's hand, which did so cruelly scourge without occasion the delicate infant," says Don Quixote.

Naturally, after the Knight rides away on Rosinante to repair other wrongs done to boys, damsels, maidenheads and widows, the farmer lashes Andrew the more.

But Don Quixote persists, enchanted always, his dream sometimes maimed by the covetous and the rout. The castle dissolves into a stale public sink only when the knavish innkeeper demands *money*, payment for the night's lodging and for straw and barley given to horse and ass. Only then does the Knight heave forth a grieved pang, "This, then, is an inn? Then I have hitherto lived in an error."

How sorrowful is the Knight's earnest entreaty when he says to Sancho, that if he will but get up on the ass and look "softly aloof" at the fleeing dust-veiled herd, he will see that the sheep, turning back to their original forms, are, as he really painted them, right, straight men!

Don Quixote must bless life, and mistake, out of naïve trust and the gentlest manners, shrewish bawds for sweet sylvaned damsels, and friar's mules for dromedaries. For whatever is villainous is incantation and error. After Sancho has been basely tossed in the blanket, as dogs are used at Shrove-tide, by the four clothiers of Segovia, the three pointmakers of the stews of Cordoba, and the two neighbors of the market of Seville, Don Quixote can only assume that such malicious sport has been practiced upon Sancho by shadows and spirits.

The devout Knight refuses to believe that there is violence in the earth, or that such clowns and miscreants are men of flesh and bone. Why, the very wounds and hurts that men give to one another are such that they can be cured by a mythical Balsam, or by a little rosemary, salt, oil and wine!

But what can Don Quixote do? What he does. "What shall we do," quoth Don Quixote, "but assist the needful and weaker side?" The first time the Knight-errant goes out in his pasted beaver trussed up with green ribbons to remove erroneous grossness, he is jocund, mirthful and expectant. Hapless knight! He is brought home, beaten to pieces, stretched out on a bundle of hay. However, the second time Don Quixote and his Squire set forth, they steal out in the night, so that none in the household or village may see how two ill-shaped curmudgeons go to engage the world in the quaintest and most ridiculous exercise of Faith!

The Quixotist must affirm what is not, Dulcinea, giants, armies, the Helmet of Mambrino, since the common mass will forever deny what IS: Don Quixote, Sancho Panza and Christ. Otherwise, life cannot be waged ideally; the cynical realism of the multitude has always been such that Christ's existence has been denied and Shakespeare has been turned into an embezzling "scientific" merchant. Does not the worldly historian, Simon Carrasco, grossly caricature Don Quixote and Sancho Panza while they live! And do not the pusillanimous conspirators, the barber, the curate and the scholar, lock up the Knight in a cage drawn by oxen, to mortify the man who would be myth? Of the rude spoilers of the gallant faith, the Knight speaks his furies, like the Fool in *Lear*, when he addresses his niece, stinking Lady the brach: "Is it possible that a piss-kitchen that scarce knows how to make bone-lace, dares to speak and censure the histories of knights-errant?"

How can truth and ideal myth prevail against those who mock man's past, his legendary memories; who say that the "love between Sir Tristran and La Belle Ysoude" is vain chimera; who basely deny the existence of King Arthur, "who goest yet about the world in the shape of a crow." For the disbeliever, no hero or noble love ever was:—and though "in Roncevalles there yet hangs Orlando's horn, which is as big as a very great joist," he perishes too, as a craven tale in the catiff mouths of the barber, the curate, and the scholar!

However, without Sancho Panza, Don Quixote perishes, nailed upon the windmills, as Christian ascetic and martyr: he dies as vainly as Christ.

Don Quixote goes out to charge heaven and man to be just, good and seemly: while Sancho, remaining at home in his ribs, marrow and skin, lets nature and necessity, cudgels, ass, horse, make the decision. Thus the Spirit mounts the winds, stars and seas as master, while the Bones sit and wait as bondsmen to chance. Whatever happens, the flesh and blood will say yea or nay to the occasion.

For Sancho, the Bones and the Servant, is the Redemption and the Master of Don Quixote, the Spirit. Flesh and Blood mock and undeceive the intellect. And Sancho doubts Don Quixote, for the Bones doubt the Head long before the Head knows.

Sancho pities and chides his Lord, his spirit and his error, and fate makes the fable. While Don Quixote holds to his fast to remain faithful to the Enchantment, the

Squire, guttling the "belly-munitions" from the wallet, is slyly arguing that beeves and partridges are "gross meats" "not befitting so noble a Knight." It is life, not virtue and morals, that makes Sancho's proverb sane and true: "The guts uphold the heart, and not the heart the guts." When Don Quixote, holy zealot himself, has over- thrown a monk whose habit Sancho cannot resist ransack- ing, the animal-longing to take and to have pilfers both Knight and incident of any piety. After Don Quixote has been locked in the cage by the barber and the curate, Sancho's most compassionate concern is whether his Grace can still pass water!

Asceticism and self-chastisement are repugnant to San- cho Panza. Will laying hands upon his buttocks recall what is lost? So when Sancho Panza does penance to Don Quixote for the disenchantment of Dulcinea by lash- ing the hedges and trees instead of his own body, he

whips the source and end of all man's sorrows, nature: for earth, famine, drought, earthquakes, women, harvests and rains, will bring the havoc, the denials, the kisses and the chastening!

Sancho Panza is good, sly, knavish, fleshly and withal a carnal liar, but he is never untrue to Sancho. Nor is he less noble than the Knight. Don Quixote also lies, about the windmills, the sheep, the cup and knight-errantry, to save his soul from the infamy of disenchantment; while Sancho's deception, coming from sensual appetite, the desire to eat well and live long, obeys Providence no less by declining to starve and flog the body the Lord gave him.

Nor can Sancho refuse or deny himself whatever God, out of heaven's vineyard and larder, offers—land, grain, fruit or geese; with these he can be bountiful, woo men, women and also receive: "To give and to have doth a brain crave." Sancho Panza will govern, if he can—" 'Tis good to command, though it be but a head of cattle,"— and obey, if he must. With a blooming appetite and heart he goes to be governor of an island, and then abdicates after a few days because he cannot eat capons, drink wine nor sleep without fear of poison. Sancho Panza leaves the Island of Barataria, that accursed and caitiff world of panders and thieves, with but a loaf of bread for himself and a little barley for his ass Dapple, because his nature cannot subsist or ripen there. He returns, unbewildered nor dismayed, to his goats, and to the tousled, russet petticoat of his wife Teresa. Life ravels out whatever happiness, goodness or honors there are; nothing comes altogether, or beforehand; ends, ideals, love, faith, happen along the way, as bypaths to hunger, guile, sex, lust. We bleed, we suffer, we know not why, and the Lord provides the vision, the altar and the lamb for Abraham: or, as

Sancho says, "God gives the wound, and God gives the salve; nobody knows what may happen."

Don Quixote dies disillusioned; to redeem human faith and courtesy he had thrown himself into delusion and trance. With a will for goodness, virtue and beauty that brought a dying delirium and derangement of his senses and organs, he delivered his affections and gospel to beasts and millsails, because the world had altogether declined his existence. Valorously he beckoned windmills to resound to his heart's fury: "Fly not, ye coward and vile creatures! for it is only one knight that assails you!" He made woodland music, a pine-mantled reverie of love and shepherdesses, out of a sowgelder's whistling of canes. He carried on hosannas, triumphal marches, combats midst the noise of trumpets, drums and horses' neighing that were but the bleating of muttons.

He invented everything, the Helmet of Mambrino, Dulcinea del Toboso, and took a Squire, a companion to be with him in his Folly till death, because he could not live in solitary contempt with barbers, curates and trollops. He addressed his Grief, which the world had so rankly abused, with the most tender civilities: "Assist me, dear lady, in this first dangerous scorn." Dante, also pitying his denials, had created a Beatrice who spoke to him in an "angelic voice," and who so modestly turned aside to weep for his torments. When Francesca tells how Paolo gave her his trembling mouth when he read of Lancelot, who kissed his lover's "fond smile," Dante faints with pity; just as Don Quixote lost reason and consciousness when he attacked the friars for imprisoning the Blessed Icon of Immaculate Mary, upon whose cheeks the Knight had seen pitiable tears!

Dante, who could not bear his scorn alone, took a guide

to accompany him, Virgil. Don Quixote, no less desperate, had as only solace and friend, Sancho Panza, "Son of my entrails."

Don Quixote had hoped to recall all men to their original arcadian state by the sweet cajolery of addressing them in a polite tongue, in the medieval meter of a ballad or a canto. He had believed that everyone is equal, only to be reminded, however, by his neighbor, whom he had saluted as Sir Roderick de Navarre, that all men are just common, of one rude, stock vision; that he, plain Peter Alonzo, was no more Navarre than Master Quixada of his own village was Knightly Quixote.

Refusing to admit that men were base, evil, knavish, he died a rueful infidel to his own soul, saying that there was no knight-errantry on all the earth. "My dear friend," says the dying Quixote to Sancho, "pardon me that I have given thee occasion to seem a fool as I was, in making thee to fall into the same error wherein I was fallen, that in the world there have been, and still are, errant knights."

Sancho Panza, however, deceiving himself the less, is the more noble. Taking the clothiers, the merchants, the lackeys for the low buffoons they are, he nevertheless follows his master into the vainest of combats; he espouses the dreams, the inventions, the phantasmal Dulcinea, though he knows they do not exist, because the brain and the spirit cannot abide life without them. And so weeping at the deathbed of his Lord, Don Quixote, he implores him to rise up and go into the field, and in the attire of a shepherd to wander under the stars, upon the hills and vales, to find Dulcinea! O Sancho! Sancho! My Flesh, my Blood, my Towers! verily how more easily does enchantment come to the grass-enamored Bones than to the stubborn, all denying Head!

VII

WOMAN

Inscribed to my very dear Friend, Charles Olson: My dear Charles: Literature, we know, is the art of ripening ourselves by conversation; and originality is but high-born stealth. How much of our talks have yeasted and bloomed this little Herman Melville loaf; and how I have played the cutpurse Autolycus, making my thefts as invisible as possible, you and my blushes best know. But here is my hand with Mephistopheles' orison: When your own polestar Truths surge upon the whited page, may "God's spies" put the same vermilion Guilt upon your face!

1. *"I WAS NAKED; AND I HID"*

Look at the New England Rebekahs, Sarahs, Isaacs, Samuels, Abigails—Hebrew savors and names—who dwelt in Ipswich, Salem, Falmouth, Truro, as in Shechem and Ai. The Hebrew used the grape, pomegranate and Lebanon cypress, for bed, table, tabernacle and Shittim Ark; while the Puritan added up his land, tillage and sweet-shingled houses into a yoke and fast for toil, Sabbath and prayer. Hebrew and Puritan multiplied: Abraham in Canaan cherished the fruit of the womb and blessed the breasts; he lay with his beloved Sarah unto her ninetieth year, when she conceived; while Pilgrim Abraham, Isaac or Samuel stealthily crept from his bed as from vice.

Abraham, Jacob, Joseph always journeyed toward the bridal East, the Jordan, Euphrates, Goshen. Joseph the Dreamer was embalmed in a coffin—so ends miraculous Genesis from the Void to Egypt. The Puritan Patriarch, however, made a New Genesis beyond Asia and Europe, in the West, turning creation, memory, fable and man, hindwards.

From the Old Testament the Hebraical Puritan took a garbled Jahweh, added to it an inclement, Atlantic Christ and a Devil, and of these made witchcraft New England— the allegory of Adam, Eve, the Serpent and Cotton

Mather. Satan's Bible, Cotton Mather's *Wonders of the Invisible World*, was the fountainhead of Puritan diabolism: *The Scarlet Letter, The Mosses, Moby Dick,* Poe's *Tales* and the poetry of Emily Dickinson—the little Puritan devils, and the vestal witch of American Literature.

All of the Puritan fantasies were unholy, libidinous quests for the WONDERS of the INVISIBLE WORLD, the wicked spermaceti, the sexual *Scarlet Letter.* Hid within the carnal-hued Letter was the concupiscent WONDER of the Privy Teat, escutcheon of Cotton Mather's witch.

For two centuries American Literature was the unresolved Riddle of the Disgrace. Poets and scribes in America were telling Satan's beads as vassals of Cotton Mather. Almost two hundred years after the Witch Trials, Nathaniel Hawthorne was denouncing the Sin of Salem in a Pilgrim scripture, *The Scarlet Letter*; Poe was steeping himself in a saturnalia of murder rites.

Herman Melville chose as the name of his tragedian the most iniquitous King Ahab from Chronicles; then he took as a second Hero an Animal, an infernal whale; clothed in the Paschal garment of the Lamb, he turned it into pure, spermal Demon.

Each one took his impious revenge against Mather's Shade, and wrote his Devil's Orison, save Emily Dickinson; fearful of the sign of the Teat, she hid in immaculate Lamb's Clothes.

Hawthorne nibbled at hell's bread, sowed evil seed, created aerial goblins and sexual scented dews in *The Mosses.* Melville shaped an antichrist Ahab, who roamed blasphemous, upboiling seas in pursuit of a Mephisto-Lamb, Moby Dick. Ahab spat into the sacramental silver calabash, uttering in final profanation a mock Lord's Prayer in Latin:

Ego non baptiso te in nomine patris, sed in nomine diaboli.

Melville broiled in ejaculatory blasphemies; of Ezekiel's Vision and Cotton Mather's Shade, he composed spermaceti Angels; of a Satanic brute, Moby Dick, he made a leering monstrance, transubstantiating creamy foams and breakers of brit and squid, Leviathan's Mead, into a wine and wafer supper.

Yet none could speak: Hawthorne could scarce mention

carnal embrace; Poe had uttered in vain, "And Sorrow shall be no more, and Eros all"; Melville made vasty, inverted oaths.

What cunning equivalents these demonic Puritan artists used to announce the body! Melville created out of a Dream an epithalamium to the Seed: "In thoughts of the vision of the night I saw long rows of angels in Paradise, each with his hands in a jar of spermaceti." He celebrated the naked living sperm; a nocturnal symbol, it was a wedding song of Moby Dick rather than the sun-leavened acclamation of the flesh. Of sea grass, drear wave-plaited oceans, he wove a nuptial bed for copulating whales. Upon his brain was painted naked, voluptuous woman; what he chanted was the milky, musky breasts of leviathan, the sexual embraces of porpoises.

Other poets have knelt before the magic of the eyes and the tresses of sweet-thighed girls: Heine sang of *Nordsee* maids; Dostoevski ached for the Foot of woman; Melville, in rapt, torn paeans, warbled the festal founts of the teats and the anus of the whale! He caroled the "delicate side fins," "the palms and the flukes," "the chaste-looking mouth," "glossy as bridal satin," and the exquisite hid leaf of ear, of Leviathan!

Melville pined for the "tinkling cow-bells in Uz," for the wells, the orchards, the flocks of Canaan, but pursued white blubber, squid, brit, ambergris. Melville gazed, as Charles Olson has said, in fervid faith and hope upon Mahomet's Crescent, the Eastern Star over Bethlehem; and roamed, as Ahab did, a finny, Topheth Pacific in a womanless whaling ship.

His life, like outcast Ishmael's, was as sundered as the crew of the Pequod in *Moby Dick*: here were two opposing human climates, sealed up in an accursed, salty hull until perdition. There were sanguinary Quaker whalers, Nantucketers, lonely Starbuck and an Atlantic atheist crew, "whelped" "by the sharkish sea" with "small touch of human mothers in them." There were Asian primal Fedellah, Afric "Ahasuerus Daggoo, imperial Negro," Polynesian Queequeg, and tropical Tashtego. These were Atlantic and Genesis men, wandering together over a boreal, brackish sea, chasing a "dumb vast sea brute" compounded of an unyeasty Jahweh, Dionysus, and the Philistine idol Dagon, to satiate the metaphysical hunger of a Puritan Devil, Ahab, "with a crucifixion in his face."

Melville ached for the Jordan, the Euphrates, those "gorgeous skirts of Asiatic land older than Abraham"; in *Moby Dick* he was Adamic Ahab, "staggering beneath the piled centuries since Paradise"; and in *Mardi* he was witness of man's Full Cycle: "I was overwhelmed in Gomorrah . . . I was at the subsiding of the Deluge . . . with the Israelites I fainted in the Wilderness. . . ."

Creation was hallowed to him: how earth, Adam, Eve, the Garden were formed; yet void and water, the Lord's First Day, were his Primal chaos—his beginning and end.

Ahab roved "sea pastures," "watery prairies," coursing through sod and swaths of ambergris, looking for Land, a jot of Nineveh or Babylon. Poe had sent out the Raven; Melville waited in vain for a returning Noah's dove with a green leaf.

Whatever Melville blessed, he refused, cursed. He had commemorated the suppers of Xerxes, Ahasuerus, Montezuma and Powhattan, but his own viands had been moldy crusts of ocean. Ahab, like Odysseus, weeping for Ithaca and Penelope, cried out for a bed, a hammock, a saddle, a sentry-box, a hearth, a pulpit, a coach—a dry snug hearse.

He worshiped an inscrutable creator, the Lord and his Son, but shaped out of an heathenish animal, a fish, flesh and fowl idol, Dagon. He adored the pure, albic vesture of gentle Christ, the fleece of White which he heaped upon the hated hump of Leviathan.

In Melville land and light are forever foresworn. Ahab, "darkness leaping out of light," prowls murdering seas of sharks and swordfish: the Night—"horrors of the half-known life." All the bodings, those stepmother intuitions, foretold in the archangelical shrieks of birds hovering above the Pequod, go unheard.

The malediction is consummated. But before the doom,

a choric lament rises up: Ahab mourns for the marriage-pillow, for green land, for the "magic glass" of the human eye; Pip pores in revery over the lilies. While the Pequod, the Atlantic World, goes down, and the musky spermaceti Angels are forever lost, Stubb, bemoaning a crusty ocean mattress-grave, cries out: "Cherries! cherries! cherries!"

The dirge is done and only Ishmael remains. A psalm and genesis of sperm, flesh and copulation, decrying celibacy, had been imagined; a Doomsday Book had been conceived.

What does *Moby Dick* portend? Is there not something drearily amiss? Here is a human, cosmological Atlantic Tragedy, without one female figure. *Moby Dick*, like Melville's watery planet, is a sundered shadow: earths and fruits are only intimated or dreamed: Ahab, Starbuck and Ishmael are ecliptic heads and torsos—woman is unguessed, uncreated. Melville made a Cosmos of evil and Satan, but without an Eve, and so composed an apocalyptic revelation without serpent wisdom.

Thoreau, "bachelor of nature," indeed! wrote of war, economy, ruminative sitting, waiting and eremitic patience, altogether excluding women, and erected in *Walden* the Western Fable of Ennui.

Poe's demonic tales never emit erotical lusts; in Emily Dickinson, the appetites, sensual throbs, were always attributes of dew, the bee, a wagon.

The books of the Puritan visionaries are the Lamb's testament; they lack the joyful knowledge that is the comedy of guile, habit, pleasure, the grape and wit of the house, the table and the bed. In the whole of Christian pilgrim literature, including the erotical saviorism of Walt Whitman, there is scarcely a laugh or a sigh, the gambol of a Puck or a faun.

Without woman, the Tree of Good and Evil cannot be tasted. Before the First Deception, Adam is Primordial Clod. The truthseekers, Jehovah and Abraham, are impotent before the froward artfulness of woman. When Sarah is told that she will sport with Abraham and conceive at ninety, her raillery at such ridiculous visionary idealism, "After I am waxed old shall I have pleasure?" is of the blood and bread of nature, custom and art.

The magnetical lodestar is man's—the cunning belongs to Sarah, Rachel and Rebekah; Sarah laughs at the Lord's guileless truth, because it contradicts experience: with a piece of goat's skin Rebekah can dupe Patriarch Isaac.

The Dreamers in the Bible, Jehovah, Abraham, Isaac, Jacob, Joseph, are male innocents! Jacob may wrestle with an Angel for Foreknowledge, but after seven years' toil in the fields of Laban for his beloved, he does not know till morning that he has slept with "weak-eyed Leah" instead of radiantly formed Rachel. Joseph, interpreter of Pharaoh's dreams, and shrewd overseer of Egypt's kine and granaries, is a gawk before Potiphar's wife.

Visions and ideals are intermixed with the pang and mirth of warming sensual lies, deceit, habit, the gossipy leaven of art, Rabelais' "cup of dissimulation."

Abstract truth is a peril: the MAN-Jehovah will destroy the Cities of the Plain for an abstraction, morals, law, righteousness; and by fire and death cleanse the sinning, slothful bones; but Woman, like Lot's wife, will look back to Sodom and Gomorrah, though she be turned into a pillar of salt.

Man, apart from woman, makes a carnage of his destiny; torn, he chases a dumb leviathan till death; he sups on a trencher of quagmire, or upon Gethsemane's grief, as Thoreau and Dickinson did. There is no such withering of man's fruits in the Psalms of the Lover, David, or in the polygamous wisdom of Solomon, or in that deep draught of grape-brewed vanity, Ecclesiastes.

Had Jesus married the illuminated prostitute, Magdalene, he would have forsaken the Acts, the overthrowing of the tables of the pigeon and money-venders, and the Bleeding Cross and given man as inheritance an imperishable generation of gentle little children or Galilean verse.

But there is no Magdalene, not even a Mary or Martha, in the Puritan Testament; woman does not exist in these literary masterpieces, in *Moby Dick*, or in *Walden*. There has never been a *Mater Dolorosa* in America, Our Lady of Succor;—those sorrowful inclined surfaces of the Primitives, upon which man saw the pity for his own pain, have never existed here. Christ, as healing "feminine" image, has always taken the place of the Virgin Mary.

For Melville Christ is the Spouse, "the soft curled hermaphroditical" Son. In Shaker theology Jesus is male and female; for celibate Rappites, He is Adam and Eve. Paul is the teacher of the bacchic Perfectionists at Oneida, and the master of the Fruitlanders is Pythagoras. For Emily Dickinson, Christ is the Bridegroom!

Melville had come to deny woman as a planetary creature. In the brief pagan heyday in *Omoo, Typee, Mardi,* he believed he had moulded nude female cannibals; in hue and shape; however, he had limned insubstantial and aerated phantoms of sensuality, Fayaway and Yillah.

After the ritual sloth and sex of Polynesia, Melville had essayed a North American *Niebelungenlied,* with the sea-dragon Moby Dick, and Ahab, as half Christian seer and half warlock.

In *Pierre* it was incest; but Isabel, the beloved of her

brother Pierre, is an air-substanced, leafy, bowered Yillah —only more Atlantic and fjord-like in speech and temper. Whatever Isabel was, as inward form in her creator's bosom, she walks upon the imaged page as Shaker sister who loves her brother in Christ! "There is no sex in our immaculateness!"—"thy nobleness unsexes me!" declares Isabel. The real "Aphroditean devotees" are Pierre and his boyhood friend. For Melville those perfervid, ideal courtesies between Paolo and Francesca, Dante and Beatrice, were more palpable between men.

No lady ever had windmills in her brains: Dulcinea del Toboso could powder porks, but never comprehend the imperial courtesies of Don Quixote's heart.

Herman Melville had turned to man for angelhood, Lamb and Christ. Of the inclement New England wife he had said: "Juxtaposition marries men"; of the troth between men: "Warm friends . . . are the Trades."

In that womanless Atlantic hull, the *Pequod*, wrathful and fissured men are always celestially courteous in their speech with one another. Pip, the Cap and Bell Fool to Ahab, as Charles Olson has identified him, is, in spirit and breeding of the heart, no less than the Fool is to Lear. Stubb's cry to his mates in dire peril is a tender exhortation: "Pull babes, pull sucklings." Queequeg, the Polynesian cannibal, makes a ceremonial of his affection for Ishmael—Queequeg "pressed his forehead against mine, clasped me round the waist, and said that henceforth we were married; meaning . . . that we were bosom friends."

In *Benito Cereno*, slave, villain and friend, show one another "courtesies even to the point of religion." Babo, mutinous Negro leader, is magisterial in his attendance upon Benito Cereno, although he is ready to cut his throat. He conceals his wily stratagems behind the most refined

obeisances! A lapse of breeding in Benito Cereno is the
cause of inward suffering to the good captain Delano.

What was Melville's quest? His insatiate hunger for
absolutes, for the Platonic Forms of gentleness, mercy and
understanding, was taking him whither?

In his pilgrimage for the "heart's virgin experience,"
Melville, in his last year, had conceived in *Billy Budd* pure
Male manhood, but had drawn a vestal maiden in the
likeness of one of Fra Angelico's seraphs.

Billy Buddy, the sailor, in complexion, charm and mod-
esty, is a girl: his name, Budd, lovely April's darling. He is
one of Shakespeare's angelical beauties of the Comedies, in
rustic attire or page's suit. But Budd's damsel features,
unlike Shakespeare's boy's garments, unmask rather than
disguise him. His "fair cheek" is like "Ruddy-tipped
daisies," his ear, small, the "arch of the foot," and "curve

in the mouth and nostril," shapely. Moreover, Billy Budd, as so many rural maids, cannot read or write: he is as illiterate as Heine's peasant wife or Goethe's Frederica, the cook.

Is Budd maid, cherub or Christ? His clothes are washed and mended by the crew with the love and piety bestowed upon the tender vestments of a girl or the sacral dress of the Virgin Mary.

Was the *Pequod* a Sodom on the seas? Did Melville, in heart's rage and obscure lust, burn, as is hinted, in the Fires of Gomorrah?

Moby Dick, Pierre and *Billy Budd,* are legends of St. Paul's "mysteries of iniquity"—Evil washed in the Blood of the Lamb. Cloven Ahab, we know, is antichrist; incestuous Pierre is "a visible token" of the "invisible angelhoods"; assassin Budd is mantled in the "fleece of the Lamb of God" when he is hanged; the spar from which his pinioned figure is suspended becomes a holy relic to the sailors who keep "a chip of it" as "a piece of the cross."

Pierre, Isabel and Budd are as chaste as Shakespeare's Miranda and Perdita, those female abstractions of purity. Shakespeare, however, had had his loafy, mealy Falstaff, his Mistress Overdone and Doll Tearsheet: in hell's heat he had unclothed Regan and Goneril; his ladies, Rosalind, Kate Hotspur and Cressida, can be full, ripe bawds. The closest Melville had come to free, ribald speech is the one line in *Moby Dick*, Quaker Captain Bildad's warning: "If ye touch at the islands, Mr. Flask, beware of fornication."

In *White Jacket* he had recited all the vices in a man-of-war, thieving, skulking, flogging and drinking; however, he had only mentioned that Cherub Man carries within him the profligacy of Ham.

Shakespeare had expired in his fifties in his Last Prayer, *The Tempest*; but Melville partook of the "penitent bread of the Supper" when he was thirty-one.

Melville had read the Poet deeply, but Backwards—in his moan, grief and prayers—"St. Shakespeare" "full of Sermons-on-the-Mount, and gentle, aye, almost as Jesus."

How quickly were the voices of Melville, Poe, Dickinson and Whitman entombed. Before the American satyr had grown his bacchic horns, he was wedded to the Holy Ghost and the Worms: Poe and Melville had fawned upon the devil, and Whitman had wrapped himself in maggots; but each one, long before he had spoken his abysses, was chanting dissolution, Poe's "Eureka," Melville's muteness, Whitman's Flower of Death, "Calamus."

In America Mephistopheles was translated into a Gothic gargoyle, to murder forever the vision of Helen. The renaissance, the legend of a mocking, European Mephistopheles and a carnal Faustus, dismally lapsed into a long Puritan *Walpurgisnacht* in which Faustus, Helen and Mephisto reappeared as medieval devils, hags, Ahab, the wicked whale.

To damn sensuality, laughter and irony, Cotton Mather had turned woman into a witch; Poe took the infernal witch, begot by Mather, and buried her alive; Melville exorcised her! Lady Dickinson hid in Christ's Bosom.

The rage of Ahab for the milky spermal substance of Primal Evil, which he pursues to murder, is the same fury that is in Cotton Mather to destroy sexual iniquity—to find the devil's excrescence, the sign of the teat!

The witch, the whale, the sperm, the teat! While Ahab chases Moby Dick upon blasphemous Sea Hells, he proclaims that it is he who is being pursued unto damnation by the Devil!

2. "THE VENOM THOU HAST POURED ON ME BE STILL, MY SPIRIT."

"Master, where is Phlegethon and Lethe found?" In the last chasm of American Literature where wails "the seraph-harper, Israfel," midst the "caitiff-choir" of those entombed women, Ligeia, Rowena, Ulalume. Poe, like Dante, addressed his moan to the Lady in Heaven; to the archangel "maid that is no more." Unlike the Poet's Lady, Poe's women are Black Angels with condor wings: their attar is the sepulcher's, their locks the raven's, and their teeth talons that belong to those obscenely nested Harpies "who chased the Trojans from the Strophades."

In the "scoriac river," the fiery tarn, or the putrid pool of Poe's Tragical Traumas, there is a runic recital of the most woeful combat between man and woman. The "angels who sob at vermin fangs in human gore imbued" are the murderesses, and the kneeling Adorer at the "vault of lost Ulalume" is the Assassin.

Poe is Al Aaraaf who swoons before the "Houri glances," wraps his grief in the holy "tresses of Annie" and sings of female angelhood, "full of odors which are the prayers of saints."

The Beloved Ones are always tenants of the "legended tomb," the worm's "moody food." Their names, Zante, Ulalume, Ermengarde, Ligeia, are of some wild clime. The abhorred ones, with the "finger of death" upon their charnel bosoms, are funeral shadows who dwell in burial-abodes, the House of Usher, or in Lady Rowena's ebon chamber. The marriage-bed, "with a palled canopy above," is always the coffin for the deposit of the beloved.

Hallowed is the obituary remembrance, "the image of

her who is no more": the Hebraical mouth of Ligeia, "the voluptuous slumber of the under lip," the Cabalistical intellect, the brow and nose, are sacred. Alive, Ligeia's erudition, Berenice's teeth, Morella's esoterical caress, are hideous phantasms.

Al Aaraaf's invocation, "And the will therein lieth, which dieth not," is a prayer which heaven denies: for Ligeia, "the august, the beloved one," has a "gigantic volition": Ligeia "doth not yield herself to the angels" "through the weakness of her feeble will"; dying, she wrestles with "grim Azrael."

And death brings no cessation: after Ligeia is in her tomb, the struggle between the two continues in her successor, Lady Rowena. The bridegroom Al Aaraaf has arranged a bridal-chamber for Lady Rowena, in each of whose "angles stands a gigantic sarcophagus of black granite." In the gruesome battle between Poe–Al Aaraaf and Rowena of Tremaine, "loathed with a hatred belonging more to demon than to man," Ligeia's ashes are wept over; Rowena is poisoned and interred alive; and while Al Aaraaf keeps a vigil at Rowena's couch, he gives himself over to "passionate waking visions of Ligeia"; Rowena, her envenomed will stronger than "the conqueror worm's," trembles.

The combat between deceased Rowena and Al Aaraaf grows fiercer; thrice she awakes from the coffin in "this hideous drama of revivification," until, lo! out of Rowena's Shadow pours forth the figure of Lady Ligeia, defying the "bandages and draperies" of the moldering grave. Al Aaraaf rushes to embrace Ligeia, begirt with "huge masses of disheveled hair" and kneels to her, "the lost love," the "beautiful one," she who is no more:

> Ligeia! wherever
> Thy image may be . . .
> Ligeia! Ligeia!
> My beautiful one.

But Ligeia, loosening the "ghastly cerements" with the will of a "tumultuous vulture," shrinks from his infernal touch.

Each woman is cloaked in the bridal-garments for her worm-nuptial—"soft may the worms about her creep." In death Eleonora and Ermengarde are seraphim whose ashes are deposited in the "censers of the angels." Only after returning from the grave does the adored skeleton, swathed in her "yet unmoldered shroud," fall into the loving arms of the bereaved husband.

Their dying, prolix and fierce, is a sickening revel of energy to enfeebled Al Aaraaf. The hair of Ligeia is a wrathful, jetty flood compared with the wan nerve-spun locks of Roderick Usher. The "phantasma of teeth" of Berenice, the agile blue veins of slowly decomposing Morella are horrible tokens of the "gigantic volition." "Shall I then say that I longed with an earnest and consuming desire for the moment of Morella's decease?"

He, "the wounded spirit of Gilead," spoils the grave to quiet the female will. He had buried Rowena alive and had violated Berenice's casket to possess the teeth! Upon Lady Madeline's coffined robes was blood, "evidence of a bitter struggle." "We have put her living in the tomb," moans Roderick Usher. But the will, that "serpent vitality" whose fumes make an eternal breach between man and woman, never dies.

When dead Ligeia comes forth she is taller; the child of deceased Morella grows monstrously in stature and in intellect! After Lady Madeline has arisen from her coffin, "lofty and enshrouded," she falls upon Roderick Usher and he expires.

The struggle never ceases. Neither the dead nor the living have repose: the vault is always open that the "mournful burden," the tenant, may never rest. In "The Black Cat" the female corpse is buried in the wall, standing; in "The Murders in the Rue Morgue," the orangutan thrusts the body perpendicular up the chimney. The deposited Lady rots erect in "The Premature Burial."

The stately, charnel-monologues, "of worms, of tombs and epitaphs," lapse into the deranged, muffled sobbings of the Black Cat, into the brutish "incoherent syllabification" of the orangutan; Al Aaraaf is changed into the loathed shape of the "large fulvous" beast that uproots the tresses and mutilates the throats and tongues of the two spinsters in the Rue Morgue.

The details of the murder of Marie Roget are orgiastic: the slip "torn upward from the bottom to the waist"; the disordered dress "beneath the frock of fine muslin"; the white petticoat "on the upper stone"; the garter, the lace embedded in the flesh of the neck. "Had the body been in any respect despoiled?" asks Dupin.

The rites of murder, interment and expiation, their portent and enigma, are revealed finally in "The Black Cat." The murder of the Black Cat is the same, in evocative horror and remorse, as the rending of Berenice's garments, "ruddy and clotted with gore"; as the struggle, unto death, between Roderick and Madeline Usher.

The apparition—"the phantasm of cat"—that bites the master is Berenice whose "ghastly spectrum of teeth" Al Aaraaf extracts!

An eye of the abhorred cat is gouged; the "unoffending brute" is hanged; but the cat returns! appallingly larger and taller, as were Morella, Ligeia and Madeline Usher after they were interred. The Black Cat is compressed into the wet substance of a wall upon which its gigantic effigy is hideously limned!

There is a Second Cat, also one-eyed, which is a hapless replica of the first: it is single identity, as are Ligeia and Rowena, Eleonora and Ermengarde, the twins Roderick and Madeline Usher, Morella and child: "I found no traces of the first in the charnel where I placed the second—Morella."

The "hideous drama of revivification" is reiterated; the Second Cat is Rowena of Tremaine, the huge Child Morella, the "lofty and enshrouded" Madeline; its pestilential being and caresses are Berenice's or Morella's odious love.

The two are one: the Second Cat, sphinx of absolute will and single, impermeable identity, is the "gigantic volition" of Ligeia, Madeline or Morella, that will not die. And the Black Cat and the wife are identical; obviously when the axe of the Master is aimed at the vile skull of the Black Cat, it cleaves the wife's brain instead!

The ritual again is the same: the cat is entombed in "brickwork behind which stood the corpse of the wife of my bosom." When disinterment supervenes, the Black Cat sits atop the corpse's head and sobs with red orbs and swollen carmined lips—the "beast whose craft had seduced me into murder."

"The will therein lieth, which dieth not."

Was Poe Mephitic? What was the ill-omened Poe? He had beseeched Heaven for *la bella Donna*; but he had sewn together in demon's threads those Furies of the Inferno which had "feet with claws, their large belly feathered."*

Poe, solitary and immured, as are all of his wailing phantoms sealed in walls, vaults or sarcophagi, looked for redemption, "surcease of sorrow," in one common, quenching, cosmical embrace. His superscription to Berenice was Plato's "itself, by itself solely, ONE everlasting, single."

"Eureka," his final threnody and metaphysic, was a grievous and fissured singleness—an "appetite for oneness." His longing was for "illimitable intuition," "utterly incognizant of path" between soul and soul—"ghastly extremes of agony are endured by man the unit, and never by man the mass," he wrote in "The Premature Burial."

"The Colloquy of Monos and Una" is a monody of cessation in which entity becomes the Autocrat Place; it

---

* Dante's *Inferno*, Canto XIII: ". . . *piè con artigli, e pennuto il gran ventre . . .*"

is the cry for the dissolution and the death-garments of almost every American Poet.

Thus read the awful, preternatural *Tales* of combat between those volitional, spectral women of North America, and the wan Al Aaraaf of the Koran, "whose heart-strings are a lute." The infernal life, like the legend, also ravels the riddle. Poe had implored the Black Star that had cursed his Muse:

> The venom thou hast poured on me
> Be Still, my spirit.

He had wrought of his ghastly denials and hunger the apocryphal Una, Annie, Eleonora: the sublunary moors, lakes, moats and the granite caskets.

Tormented by the woeful distortion of identity, the "fierce energy" of Woman, he had married a child. Fearful of strange, unknowable blood, he had wed his cousin, and to consummate the *Tales*, she had died before becoming a preter-human, volitional Ligeia, Morella or Madeline.

In letters of funereal grief and tears, he had prayed for succor; but what had come to feed upon his own spirit was a Raven!

There is mirth, too, in Edgar Poe, the critic, and an odd and poignant gaiety. Poe's intemperate criticism of those male amateur Parnassians of his own day was wholly accurate; his wayward praise of female authors, however, was profuse gallantry.

The "Marginalia" and "Literati" were impudent diatribes on Whittier, Emerson, Bryant, Lowell, the "Quacks of Helicon," astrological fakirs with asses' blood—"Mr. Longfellow and other Plagiarists."

Edgar Poe's "Autography" was a bizarre, charlatan horoscope of the Handwriting of Poets: William Cullen Bry-

ant's "daybook and ledger" chirography, Greenleaf Whittier's boorish "clerk's hand," Fenimore Cooper's sloven "unformed penmanship." The moody ciphers of lady-poets, however, were sibylline sighs.

Edgar Poe's cavalier reviews of female authors were surreptitious valentines. In each critical tribute "the "seraph-harper, Israfel" was wooing an Unknown Heart.

How droll and sorrowful it is to hear again the names of those Venus-poetasters whom Poe, asking for paradisaical bounties never given, called Geniuses! May Edgar Poe be shriven; and may those ashy bosoms of Ladies Osgood, Whitman, Carey, Welby, Hewitt, Lucy Cooper, Sigourney, remain in Limbo!—*Resquiescat in Pace.*

Edgar Allan Poe was a saturnine and evil-mocked Saul. Of a seemly brow and of an august temperament, he was anointed a Monarch-Poet, but a malignant Star was upon him. Like anguished King Saul, who lost Israel when he tore the skirts of the Prophet Samuel, Poe's Genius was a forfeited Kingdom.

3. "SING O BARREN"

Poetry, novels, and tales, in America, were the "dialogue between the spirit and the dust"; and beneath this death-humming threnody was Ennui.

The body was inverted, as well as images of animals, objects or nature: Thoreau's "teats of Nature's pine-clad bosom"; Emily Dickinson's "wagon's stomach"; or, think! the "dimple in the tomb."

Emily Dickinson's nectar was the "julep of the bee." A "debauchee of dew," she reeled upon air.

Spinster Dickinson, tying her hat and creasing her shawl, "smoothed a homely pain" and "plaited the residue of woe with monotony"; "bachelor of Nature" Thoreau, defrauded tedium by writing bleak journals about loon,

heron and osprey: "saw teal and widgeons"; "flocks of grayish . . . speckled ducks."

Poe, Melville and Dickinson were occult wizards of allegory, never the whole human artist; Poe's voice was immured; Melville's, after *Moby Dick*, bemuted; Dickinson's wrapped in a burial cloak. The resurrection of speech came in Walt Whitman.

An obese, prophetic, fragrant man, with heavy-lidded eyes, pink, gospular face, and gaudy, swollen pieties—as Thomas Eakins had painted him—announced, "I am the true Bread." Out of Jesus' mouth he took his most equivocal parable—"For my flesh is meat indeed, and my blood dwelleth in me and I in him"—and made of it a seminal New Testament.

He took the Bleeding Nails, the Phallus, "the lung-sponge, the stomach sac," and composed a bible for Adam and Eve of the States.

He wrote a dithyrambic lexicon of all the modest and surreptitious members of the body, male and female; "scented herbage of my breast," "the womb, the teats, nipples, breast milk." All that was furtive in corporeal moisture, odor, breath, kiss or coition, became a public liturgy; "the scent of these arm-pits, aroma finer than prayer," "billowy drowse" in "amorous wet," sexual thrum of "climax and close," "the bowels sweet and clean," "orbic flex of mouth . . . filling me full," "quivering belly of love," "white blow and delirious juice."

> I believe in the flesh and the appetites;
> Seeing, hearing, feeling, are miracles.

Whitman's vision included and denied the Crucifixion, Satan, the Tragic Myth: he sounded gongs for Barabbas and Christ: all were equal, man, woman, Jesus, thief, Pilate, prostitute or venereal citizen.

Walt Whitman, the multitudes, "you flush with myself," had the uddered juice and milk of brotherhood, love, sympathy, affection; all partook alike of the Meal of democratic fraternity.

From the Galilean Whitman borrowed the Cup, the Cross and the Last Thirst; and elevated the scum and lees of the "divine average," the morals, habits, manners, progress, science, even the Constitution, into a Passion Play of the American Republic.

Nazarene, Evangel, State Shaman of sexuality, he dilated male and female citizens—"I am jetting the stuff" "of more arrogant republics." He sat with publicans, sinners, "cleaners of privies," "the venerealee" or prostitutes— "I will not exclude you till the sun excludes you." Reenacting the miracles at Bethesda, he ejaculated: "Lovers of me, bafflers of graves," "corpses rise, gashes heal, fastenings roll from me." And at the Last Supper of the True Bread, "The Song of Myself," he urged simple, blighted Peter, mechanic, cordwainer, farmer of These States, to understand Jesus' words—"Who eateth not my flesh and drinketh not my blood, he hath not eternal life."

Whitman's Miracles at Bethesda for the sexual cripples, mendicants, paralytics, the lazar-fleshed Magdalenes, Puritans, the impotent, were real. But his five loaves and two fishes never became a parable of Spirit.

Whitman's Cross, ignominy and self-abasement, like his afflatus, "Walt Whitman, am I, a Kosmos," was gorged. He hungered for every pain—"I am the hounded slave, I wince at the bite of the dogs," "Agonies are one of my changes of garments." He thirsted for degradation, but rationally drank his gall and vinegar out of the Sufferer's

Cup. For Walt Whitman never knelt, sweating drops of blood, on a Mount of Olives.

Of a drab, mammon-fed America, with a middle-class, infidel Cross, a Laodicean Church of Democracy that was neither hot nor cold, he created an amative Saviorism. Whitman's *Leaves*, a lyric manifesto on anatomy and hygiene—"heart-valves," "sexuality, maternity"—like Marx's *Kapital*, fails as myth and tragic ideal. They are canons of physiology, or a class-conscious invocation—"Give us this day our daily bread"—that never became poems for man in upheaval.

The communal "I" in the Whitman Chant cannot be a substitute for personal grief. The Word, Who suffers and bleeds upon the nails of the crucifix, is never to be compared with the redemption of the "stomach-sac," "the palate-valves," the rationalistic salvation of an abstract impalpable Class. Credos that are added to man's pulse as was Christ and Golgotha to Whitman's *Leaves*, do not reflect affliction, blood, identity.

Whitman's Mass "I" is the cold, algebraical multitude, and his "evangel-poem of love and comrades" is a Quaker abstract Adam and Eve. There is not one individual woman, name, face or dress; no Bathsheba's hair to catch a David; no Abigail, or Homeric handmaidens.

In what delicate lace and embroidery is Mary dressed; Mary, Holy Mother and Angel, is the graven-image to kneeling, medieval man, the master! But look upon those "free" women in the Edenic phalansteries, those nameless, hueless beings, brothed, bedded and seamed alike. Celibate Shaker women, married Quakeresses, Fruitlander wives, polygamous females at Oneida, all wore the Puritan bonnet, the nunnish lace-cap, the soap-scoured bloomers. Those bloomers, clean, neuter raiment, were a defamatory rejection of the difference between woman's rondured body, and man's. Is it not written in Deuteronomy, "The woman shall not wear that which pertaineth unto a man"?

With the emancipation of woman came the dethroning of Mary, and the denial of her sexual dominion. The women who dwelt in those gloomy, legislative, communistic cloisters, equal to man, were water and spirit Marthas. The medieval pacifists, Anabaptists and Moravians, in Bohemia, who practiced "communism in love," looked upon the bed as a racial vat; the Elders, like the American Perfectionists at Oneida, arranged marriages; among the latter, sexual passion was governed by a fiat.

In America, among the free, amative thinkers, Beecher, Noyes, and Whitman, Holy Writ has always been invoked before partaking of the carnal meal. Whitman sat at the erotical Last Supper in Christ's Bosom; he who chanted gluttonous feeding, winebibbery, amorous aches, was an evangelical bachelor till death.

Walt Whitman was dual, and all of his sexual imagery, even as Christ's, "This is my Body; take ye and eat," is the ache for the Pharisee's Kiss. No woman ever wiped or washed Whitman's feet with her hair; no adoring Magdalene anointed him with oil of spikenard.

Rationalists and Christian dogmatists, Socrates, Kant, Whitman, all are despisers of women: Kant's and Whitman's celibacy was a token, as it always is, of man's miserly withholding of his love and seed from woman.

Socrates, in the Prison Scene before taking the hemlock, hurries Xantippe and the weeping baby away; his effigy, like Whitman's, was man: the locks of Phaedo, the tears of Critias; Whitman's disciples were Horace Traubel, John Burroughs, Dr. Bucke.

Loving woman by precept and dogma as he did sex,

vice, chastisement, even life—"O I think it is not for life I am chanting here my chant of lovers"—Whitman did not have the wisdom, the cunning of feeling, the impious apostasy, of a European artist. Whitman craved insult and self-abasement; he thirsted for galling humiliation, in declamatory, rational sobs,—"O Christ! This is mastering me!," "I am the man—I suffer'd—I was there." He hungered for dirt, for foulness, for the muck of Job, the worms of Lazarus, for the "drunkard's breath, unwholesome eater's face" that were not his by nature or inheritance.

Whitman's *Leaves*, a Protestant teetotal gospel, had no abysses: "there is no evil," he said. A believer in the Savior, he rifled Christianity of original sin, just as the rational Perfectionists had done. By taking original sin out of Hebraic Christianity, Whitman disavowed pitiable human folly—how Absalom loved his locks, how base Caiaphas and Pilate were, how weak Peter was—and so annulled redemption. He annihilated the Savior, the Word, the Image, without which the world becomes an insensate medley of hideous flying atoms: the mock monstrance and mass of a sinister machine and a transfigured rabble.

To deny evil is to deprive the bones of penance and to shed for ever the cry of Abel's blood, the existence of Saul, Sodom, the sin of Lot's daughters, Judas Iscariot. However man may come to Being and Deity, the poor, panting Word, or absolute, suffering atheism—to refuse What Is in man, his most perfidious whoring tumults, is to steal his grace. Do not all the saints in Dostoevski's novels drop to their knees before holy, inscrutable evil; so kneels Father Zossima to the lusting Karamazovs; and so Tihon, the priest, confesses the demon Stavrogin in *The Possessed*. He who enters the swine to cast out the devils, that he may sit at the feet of Christ in sweet, white vesture, is Dostoevski's saint.

Dostoevski's free-thinkers, revolutionists or nihilists, burn lamps before icons, and die taking the sacrament. The murderer, ravisher and disbeliever, Stavrogin, is tortured by the "derisive rational devils"; "I believe," says Stavrogin, in the long nocturnal whisper between him and Tihon, "in a personal devil, not in an allegory." Doubt does what Christ cannot do, when he breaks the small ivory crucifix between his raging, tortured, doubting fingers; just as the anarchist Bakunin, who assassinated God, recreated him when he proposed putting the Sistine Madonna on the wall of besieged Dresden to protect the city from Prussian bombs! This is the penultimate frenzy, the wrestling with No-thing for Being. "I believe," jets the black yea-murmuring blood: "forgive thou my unbelief," mocks the rational, assassin brain.

He, who came to liberate anatomy, man and woman, rationally laughed at Death, nature's tragic course—"I laugh at what you call dissolution"—returned to the charnel dirge, to Poe's, Melville's, Dickinson's "My little grave a cottage is." In his joyful, primal strength Walt Whitman wrote his "Tomb-leaves," "Calamus," the Asphodel of These States.

At what peril did Walt Whitman reject what always was and must be? Giordano Bruno, a true awakener, had said, "He who impedes Nature in her course is impious and insane."

Whatever had been a sepulcher and a cause for weeping was in Whitman a chant of dilation. Koheleth in Ecclesiastes lamented that love, pleasure, work are a brief vanity, and a striving after wind; Whitman lamented not. Shakespeare and Tolstoi bemoaned that which forever cheats man of his brain, consciousness and faith; Whitman bemoaned not. The angry Prophets rebuked the multitude who love not goodness and wisdom; Whitman elevated them.

The Leaves of Grass is a hymeneal dictionary of taboo sex words; it is a testament, not of our pentecost or our fruits, but the lean issue of drought. *Leaves of Grass* is the Song of Our Barrenness, "Sing O Barren."

A gifted aboriginal, a large, ignorant Pathfinder in a brand-new Jerusalem, Walt Whitman was Balaam's Ass braying Angel Truths.

4. "FALSE, CRESSID!
FALSE, FALSE, FALSE!"

Which way revolves the wheel of Fire? Goaded by Scorpius, mountains, seas and wars, man is the First Cause of the towns, battles, women, barley-cakes, of which he is also the effect. In some rotating aeons, preying upon himself the less, he is sustained by gods, ambrosia, libations, nymphs, Ilium; his art, tools, craft and maidens are heaven's host.

The Harp of David, the song "Moab is my washpot," the flowery sorrows of Orcus, are his race-nuptials, and the holocaust of flesh at the end of *The Odyssey*, his blight and revulsion.

Which way turns the Cryptic Wheel? backwards or forwards? A single noble rite, custom, in Genesis, in *The Iliad*, becomes a future Golden Age. The Patriarch in Genesis has a breeding of the heart befitting Angels when he hurries from his tent to give the three Strangers drink, dates and lamb. How good is Abigail, who, with modest homage, brings to David two hundred loaves, five dressed sheep, two bottles of wine, figs and five measures of parched corn. What a pledge of Orphic graces is she whose girdles, garments and cloaks are put into a chariot and drawn by mules. This maid in *The Odyssey*, like Abigail, sweetly breathes the mysteries of her occupations. The women of all the golden eras are servitors and sirens; handmaidens unto man, they bathe him in water from silver ewers, anoint him in moist oil from golden cruses, knowing that the man so served is easily beguiled. They

comfort him with mast, acorns, pale honey and Pramnian wine, as Circe gulled the sailors of Ulysses.

The stratagems of women Homer knows. In *The Iliad* does not wise Minerva chatter in the bare branches in the shape of a vulture? The matronly siren Calypso uses girdles and veils to detain Ulysses: Circe awes the simple oarsmen with dogs and lions; "crafty Penelope" deceives her stupid suitors for twenty years with a loom and a distaff.

Woman, beflowered or coarsely wrought, is the vessel of man: Penelope is as "prudent" and wily as Ulysses; Persephone is as "dread" as her consort Pluto. Though Calypso be empowered by all the guile of the Homeric Greeks, she also possesses their Delphic worship of tools, artisanship, edibles. When her ruses fail, Calypso gives Ulysses an auger, a sharp steel axe with a fine handle of olive wood with which he can cut the ribs, beams and pegs for a ship. When Ulysses departs, he is clad in perfumed garments and provided with a skin of black wine and a wallet of food. Calypso's possession of magical tools is the reverence of her age for the artisan. Hesiod tells the farmer to use his hoe while praying to Zeus for crops. The shade of the sailor implores the companions of Ulysses to erect his tomb on the hoary shore and fix upon it the oar with which he rowed when he lived.

Calypso's large person, her bounteous nature, is redolent of the alder, poplar and cypress: of "leafy Pelion" and of joyful horse-pasturing Argus.

Homer's ideal women are deep-bosomed; he says that Penelope's hand was "plump," but not "thick" or "crass." William Morris's vision of a utopian socialism was a society of opulently fleshed Titian women with sheaves of ripe hair—man's "rosy-fingered morning."

Shakespeare is more harassed and baffled than Homer by woman's deceits; after the Trojan War, Menelaus, stale and impotent, lives with Helen, her bloom long since ransacked by Paris. But Troilus, the cuckold, is doomed to rage at "False Cressid."

The Patriarchal morning of Abraham and Homer has vanished. Woman is no more the servant and handmaiden of man: Antony, Hamlet, Macbeth, Lear and Troilus, are tormented, unsated slaves. Cressid and Cleopatra remain sealed and illegible characters because neither Troilus nor Antony ever mastered them. They are paradigms for the modern, complex Hedda Gablers, for Dostoevski's clair-voyant harpies.

Sarah we know; Hagar's despisal of Sarah's barrenness we grasp; but Goneril's unmilked malice, Lady Macbeth's galled breasts, surpass the ken of man. Shakespeare is as infant as Troilus, as naïve as the Fathers of human fable. So simple were the signs of nature that disclosed courtesy and grace in a woman that Abraham's servant, seeking a wife for Isaac, chose the first woman who gave him and his flocks water from the well. With an offering of dates and parched corn Abigail divulged her ample, sensual nature to David.

The most obvious artifices that Shakespeare employs betray bewilderment: Iago's snares, Lear's foolishness, are man's amazement; Hamlet's surmises are a boiling over of suspicion, for his grief tells him that Ophelia has been *hatched* by Polonius. Troilus's "false, false, false" is never more than heartbreak guess which he never comprehends. Othello's act is the result of doubting a transparent Desdemona. The Bed, hallowed by Homer, is cobwebbed during Ulysses' absence; but in Shakespeare's Tragedy, Desdemona is suffocated by the pillow upon which another head

may have lain! Shakespeare finally brought an end to the pain and the paradox by creating pure, Christian abstractions of chastity!

Rahab, Jezebel and Delilah are whores who do not mire the furies in the blood: unfaithful Helen is a prophetess in aged Menelaus's house; much-woo'd Penelope is a gracious, sturdy matron.

Woman is the sweet, opiate weed for which Othello aches and murders, the voluptuous infinite variety upon which unsated Antony feeds, Troilus's False Cressid, Lady the brach, reechy Regan and Goneril, Lady Macbeth, Volumnia, iron-bowled Mother of state-suckled Coriolanus.

The horns that gently sprout upon Menelaus's brow are a filthy cross of cuckoldry for Shakespeare. Old or young, the Shakespearean hero vents his heart's choked clamor in the most deranged curses; his tragedy lurks in the belief, inkily apprehended, that his name will be ridiculously infamous as an "oblique memorial of cuckolds." Lear, Timon, Hamlet disburden their tongues as though their marriage-sheets had been defiled; Timon, like an injured spirit in the fields of Asphodel, babbles, "Quell the source of all erections," though those who devoured him were men, not women; foolish, barren Lear howls, "Dry up in her the organs of increase." Lear's invectives against his "pelican daughters" have the ranging, spilling license of Hamlet, the lover. Hamlet's mother's sin is a promise of Ophelia's character; Ophelia is Hamlet's gnawing rage. When Hamlet paints procreation and conception as the Kiss of putrescence, he is but spewing forth his own sexual ferocities:

> For if the sun breed maggots . . . being a
> God-kissing carrion, Have you a daughter?

There is no anger at Polonius: nor is Hamlet obsessed with murder when the Play is given to bait the conscience of the king. He is in the gripe of Ophelia, and all his bawdy talk on maidenheads, his sharp puns on groans, is sexual misery. Lear despises "dog-hearted" woman. In *Hamlet* woman is man's carrion appetite; and in *Lear*— "The fitchew, nor the soiled horse, goes to 't in such nauseating riot"—man's consort only in the "deed of darkness"; so how fitting it is that Othello should be a blackamoor!

Only fops, rogues, whoresons and soldiers are salacious bed-food for Regan, Goneril, Cleopatra or Hamlet's mother: goodness is dreamy, infatuate dotage, as Lear is to his daughters, or as is honest old-fleshed Gloucester whose eyes are put out at Regan's command. Albany is "milk-liver'd" to venereous Goneril, and Hamlet is "pigeon-liver'd."

In Dostoevski's *The Gambler*, it is the French coxcomb, de Grieux, who is bitter rhapsodical food for the intellectual Polina; even the mercenary, swarthy courtesan, Mlle. Blanche, wholly despises the Gambler's money and favors until he has learned the cancan; she tries to imagine him as a voluptuous confection by dressing and cravating him like a dandy.

The Western man of ennui is the heir of the fat dregs of Hamlet's sexual sickness. "O God! I could be bounded in a nutshell . . . were it not that I have bad dreams" is the malady of boredom of the European, of Pascal, Dostoevski, Tolstoi, Stendhal. The misery and punishment of the modern spirit is that it is as doomed as Satan:

> From going to and fro in the earth,
> and from walking up and down in it.

To Pascal, stir and space were the vanity and sin of the

Occident; Stavrogin in *The Possessed* would "put gunpowder under the four corners of the earth" to quench his tedium; his craving to be deported to Siberia, to hang himself, is the hunger of Hamlet for absolute rest in Limbo. Hamlet and Stavrogin steep themselves in dreamy, mystical revulsions; the killing of Polonius is an involuntary act of beatific disgust; Stavrogin's marriage to a splenetic, crippled idiot is an act of rapture; a revolting martyred wedlock to a human deformity, it is an ecstatic hiss of profanation. Hamlet defiles Ophelia by anathematizing conception. Those who have devils in them are the unpossessed Hamlet, Stavrogin, the Priest Tihon, Lear, Timon. Each canonizes his own nausea: Stavrogin when he confessed the vile, nether filths of his soul to Tihon; and the Priest Tihon is devil and saint when he establishes a canonical hierarchy of crimes: "I will forgive you, if you also forgive me," whispers Tihon, casting out the devils and the swine of the profligate, weary heart of both priest and murderer, believer and infidel.

None so spitefully play upon these rootless heretics and free-thinkers, Hamlet, Lear or Dostoevski's characters, as the "advanced" women at whose feet they sensually exhaust themselves. None so despise themselves as the nihilists: "I am a sick man . . . I am a spiteful man . . . I am an unattractive man" is the opening line in Dostoevski's *Notes from the Underground*. The clerk who says this is so soiled and ugly to himself that he basely insults the prostitute who loves him in order to purify her! And does not cursing, wooing Hamlet, when he is erotically deranged, appear before Ophelia in muddy, ill-smelling clothes? Shatov in *The Possessed* is absolutely beside himself when the woman comes to his rotting, moldy room for a morsel of food and a bed in which to bear another man's child.

The venery of Hamlet, the "refuse embraces" of Cleopatra upon which Antony cannot sup enough, the libertine morsel Cressid, who has been so meagerly tasted by Troilus, are repeated in the ravaging amours of Dostoevski's characters. The delirium in Shakespeare's and Dostoevski's men for women is unendurable carnal misery. These are mad, unfed men in whom thronging, beating appetite can find no remedy, nor satiety an end. There is swollen erotical dementia in Shakespeare's "bugle eyeballs," in those "bluest veins" which Antony lipped. As Rosalind, in *Much Ado About Nothing*, says, "Love . . . deserves . . . a dark house and a whip as madmen do"—it

is the lash that Rosalind in *Love's Labour's Lost* would use
to make Biron beg and fawn, "And shape his service
wholly to my hests." Man must be her slave, toadstool,
fool. Dostoevski's Polina cannot make the Gambler crawl
enough; this mean, helpless toady, raving with desire, has
"only to remember and imagine the rustle of (her) dress,
to be ready to bite off (his) hands." The only men who
can torment the sensual women of Dostoevski are, if fops
and varlets be lacking, epileptics and madmen; and only
the lame and the insane are satisfying as excruciating self-
abasement for the bedeviled men. In each other they find
a visionary seizure. The lunacy of Myshkin, "Knight of the
Sorrowful Countenance," is a stinging rapture for the
demented Alexandrovna Phillipovna: of course, Myshkin,
her savior, goes to the insane asylum. The humbling of
that broken, mock, wastrel Quixote, Stephan Trofimovitch,
on his deathbed, is an ecstasy for Varvara Petrovna. Stephan Trofimovitch has nothing left but her abuse; and he
whose last wretched soul-roots were in Varvara's loving,
hating nails, dies, when he is no longer upon her malignant
crucifix, imploring: "Oh, I wish her to smite me on the
other cheek!" He is a crawling flunky to the slow, mutinous
sound of her clothes, and to the short fetching of her
breath.

> Let not the creaking of shoes
> Nor the rustling of silk betray thy
> poor heart to woman . . .

Edgar admonishes decrepit, wracked Lear!

> Fie, fie upon her!
> There's language in her eye, her cheek, her lip
> Nay, her foot speaks; her wanton spirit looks out
> At every joint and motive of her body.

O what penance and suffering remorse does Shakespeare, greatest of all the hapless menials of woman, pour forth: "What potions have I drunk of Siren tears."

That ravening, monogamic passion for women comes upon man when she is no longer in his possession. Desdemona is an Oriental heirloom, a divinely docile chattel, not modern Italian; but the Moor is the European cuckold, writhing in a hot seethe of jealousy, when he confesses that he would have preferred the whole camp, not one, to have tasted her. Othello is the continental Antony, brewed in an Elizabethan's brain—a gloomy, bitten, vituperative Antony who can never forget that when he met Cleopatra she was "a morsel cold upon dead Caesar's trencher." Sexual agenbite is a modern sickness, not Biblical; Leah, though she will offer Rachel mandrakes in order that she may lie with Jacob, has no objections to sharing her husband with Rachel. Adultery is a sin, but if a man has flocks and provender, and if he obeys the statutes, he can have several wives; David had Michal, Abigail, Bathsheba, and Solomon had an opulent seraglio.

In Homer all love is aromatic. So sanely joyful were these guzzling Olympian gods that, whenever they took sexual delights in their own beds or in a cuckold's, the dew that fell upon the whole earth was indistinguishably ambrosial.

Shakespeare, Poet of the ruined blood, longed, even in the gay, licentious comedies, for "A woman, that is like a German clock." Shakespeare believed that what he desired in woman was an elegiacal rural repast of graces and kisses, sheaved together with "russet yeas and honest kursey noes." As simple as Troilus, he himself was "weaker than a woman's tear." How frail and grateful is man for whatever dainty, smiling bounties a woman may vouchsafe him is disclosed in the delight Erasmus took in telling how the English women embraced their guests before they left; how much honey flowed out of Montaigne's pagan pen that never issued from his vixen-wife's tongue; he relished saying that "Pythagoras his neece was wont to say, that a woman which lies with a man ought together with her petiecoate leave off all bashfulness, and with her petiecoate, take the same againe."

Great Occidental literature is the Apocalypse of Tedium: this is the Night of Christ and Beast of Dostoevski. Dostoevski's novels, the blood-clad darkness which he shed, are the Western World. Dostoevski's voluptuary nihilists, the famished prophets of nonexistence, are the harbingers of the European biped who moodily fattens upon his own thwartings. He is the possessed Kirilov who asserts the godhead of his free will by suicide; he seeks redemption through absolute extinction. He is the revolutionary, world-convulsionist, who drinks the bloody footprints of men for the regeneration of society.

The craving for a dark age is eternal: the Apocalyptic Whore who comes to save man is the rotting, pullulating Attila, Tamberlaine or Hitler of his own devouring blood. The storm trooper is but the decayed tempest of self-loathing. Darkness is ubiquitous: the communist machines that free the enlightened Russian proletariat are the rational devils that obsessed the revolutionist, Stavrogin: the machinery he has heaped upon his steppes and wheat is the spewing forth of his own sickness. Petersburg, Dostoevski's or Stalin's, is the cold, rational, theoretical city —the megalopolitan ditch in which the abstract biped overpoweringly rots, alone. This national disjunctive Onan, separated from woman, whose angelical sap has been drained by the insane drudgery of industrialism, inevitably

spills his seed into the Fatherland, for rebirth! The whole
cataclysm, for a national kitchen Gretchen, for a "German
clock," is the result of this ferocious breach between the
nomadic halved male and the hyphenated worker-female.
The buxom carnal peasant-girl, the servant maid, who fed
the depleted aristocracy, now nourishes the machine and
the office: she is the splenetic manikin, with the worm-
wood of pistons, lathes, cement upon her starveled dugs
—or the lesbic free-thinking political ideologue. The de-
scendants of Dostoevski's women are sexual cripples, insane or consumptives—like the nihilist Hedda Gabler ready
to kill herself because childbirth is loathsome. Tolstoi, who
rebuked Dostoevski because his men always sinned with

women who had sickly pancake breasts, expressed the sexual tumult: "Man survives earthquakes, epidemics, the horrors of disease, and all the agonies of the soul, but for all time his most tormenting tragedy has been, is, and will be—the tragedy of the bedroom."

Dostoevski, Tolstoi and Verhaeren deeply distrusted the most carrion of mare's nests, logic: Dostoevski and Tolstoi believed in the genius of absurdity, even stupidity; Verhaeren, "swaddled in tedium," flogged his own self-gulling brain:

> The Corpse of my Reason
> floats on the Thames.

Through a ridiculous valiance, man could return to woman and vision. Does not Maria Rilke disgorge rationalism by one haughty question, a sylvan and river purification of the massacred earth-heart: "What will you do, God, when I die?"

Rilke restored Woman to her Grace by making her Angel in his *Mariensleben*, an act of celestial guilt and penance, like Hamlet's "The fair Ophelia! Nymph, in thy orisons, be all my sins remembered." Man cannot woo in woman the leafy heavens, the windy burgeoning meadows, brooks and stars, until she is the ADORATION, whom man— a Rilke sorrowed by the Fates, but beloved of the Muse— can apostrophize: "Who, if I cried, would hear me among the angelic orders?"

VIII

SUPERSTITION AND IMAGES

1. THE WITCH'S CAULDRON

The penultimate superstition of mankind is the State, and until the state has been rejected man will be a slave to darkness and ignorance: for fatherland, nation, country, patriotism, government are all black magic brewed in the witch's cauldron of World History. The State Conscience, like its founders, Remus and Romulus, has always been suckled by wolves, or, as Machiavelli writes: "You must know there are two ways of contesting, the one by law, the other by force; the first method is proper to men, the second to beasts; but because the first is frequently not sufficient, it is necessary for a prince to understand how to avail himself of the beast and the man. This has been figuratively taught to princes by ancient writers, who describe how Achilles and many other princes of old were given to the centaur Chiron to nurse, who brought them up in his discipline; which means solely that, as they had for a teacher one who was half beast and half man, so it is necessary for a prince to know how to make use of both natures, and that one without the other is not durable."

Can anyone mistake the Shakespearean historical plays, those hearse-plumed pageants of kingly knavery? Or misdoubt those tragical cozeners, thieves and land-lechers, those royal cousins and uncles of King Richard the Second? Richard himself is a demon with State bowels and liver: he steals and banishes, without spleen, without melancholy, without remorse: "Now, put it, God, in the physician's mind to help him to his grave immediately!" utters Richard, waiting to seize the dying Gaunt's moneys and estates.

Bolingbroke is the same. It is not Bolingbroke's fatherly grief that makes him deplore his son as an alehouse varlet and cutpurse-highwayman: it is policy. Bolingbroke is an iron integer: he is unfleshed lust, inconceivably *trans-human*. After he has had Richard assassinated, it is not Bolingbroke's deed, but his speech to the hireling that monsters his crime:

> I hate the murderer, love him murdered.
> I'll make a voyage to the Holy Land
> To wash this blood off from my guilty hand.

Bolingbroke will follow and mourn at Richard's bier: he will kneel before the catafalque of the State. Thus do crowns and thrones live and flourish.

One of the great mock lines in literature is Octavius Caesar's, the scarce-bearded boy's words to Cleopatra: ". . . for Caesar cannot live to be ungentle." Caesar cannot live otherwise. The boy is already an adept in the mysteries of the body politic: he *acts* his lines with state-dolor and decorum. When the great Antony, that Arabian bird who had nestled so close to Cleopatra's warm and fertile bosom, is dead, Caesar knows his Roman grief, and what mottoes are in these words, inscriptions for minted gold coins:—"the death of Antony is not a single doom: in his name lay a moiety of the world." Caesar gives the royal pair an imperial funeral: their bodies are delivered to dark, dreamless oblivion, but their souls are chronicled on marble tablets for the superstitious vassal eyes of the plebians.

Shakespeare's "political" dramas are histories of ex-sanguious wills: of Caesar's, Richard's, Bolingbroke's, Macbeth's. The heart has been bled to death by Policy-Lust.

But Shakespeare's Last Orison, *The Tempest*, is:

> I' the commonwealth I would by contraries
> Execute all things; for no kind of traffic
> Would I admit; no name of magistrate;
> Letters should not be known; riches, poverty
> And use of service, none; contract, succession,
> Bourn, bound of land, tilth, vineyard, none;
> No use of metal, corn, or wine, or oil;
> No occupation; all men idle, all;
> And women too, but innocent and pure;
> No sovereignty;—

However, the politicals of "scientific" Gehennas still give the evil eye to Shakespeare's "utopian" dream, and the jeer at the Poet is still the victory of the State.

2. STATUTE ANSWER AND MAN QUESTION

Man has "progressed" from magic to religion, and from alchemy to science: he has renounced sorcery, incantation, and totemic deities for gods and a first cause. The medieval and Romanesque cathedrals are the most inspired barbarism of European civilization: Cologne and Chartres attain such demiurgic reaches by their art that we are prone to forget, as we look at the arches, the apse, the clover-shaped stained glass, the haze-tinted seraphs, that this immense stone shadow-show is a desperate garbling of first principles: that metaphysic and art pander to idolatry and fears. Whether Spengler's art-judgment is correct or not, his observation is exceedingly true when he writes that "the terrible figures of the Romanesque cathedral-porches in France . . . are not 'art' but fear turned to stone."

If this sculptured demonology rewarded man's eye, it also befogged his brain and pumped black occult juices into his heart. The vulgar recondite mysteries of the church were for the people: the carnal gargoyles and devils were engines of admonition and intimidation. The church which transcended Reason returned man not to the heart but to terror.

The church has been as pragmatic as the state. Christianity adopted the Logos, the mithraic bull ritual, Osiris, Jupiter, Zeus, and transformed them into the Word, the crucifixion and the resurrection, just as readily as Constantine made Christianity a state religion. Church and state became inseparable: king, pope, and Borgia were one and three and forever related. Papal skulduggery and Borgian poison, dagger and fratricide went hand in hand: the host could not be reviewed without the dagger. The church could not continue without Caesarism. The Rock of Peter rested upon history and not upon personal belief. Pilate washes his hands of the Truth before him so that History can continue. Spengler writes, "*World-history is, and always will be, State-history.*" The tragic struggle between Caesar and the Word *is* eternal.

Shakespeare, who is a secular poet, never fails to attack superstition, Roman law, kingship, nepotism, necromancy, caste, class and Caesarism. Witness in *Measure for Measure* the comic decree against non-juristic sexual intercourse. Claudio is to be executed because he has bedded illegally his fair Juliet (imagine any other kind of bedding). How Lucio bawds these sweet necessities and what a mirthful measure he takes of the governor, Lord Angelo, false savior of the maidenheads of the realm! What a teacher is the Elizabethan sibyl, the whore Mrs. Overdone:

> Thus what with the war, what
> With the sweat, what with the gallows and
> What with poverty, I am custom-shrunk.

Macbeth is a study in the Gothic superstitions of the state. The play's not in Macbeth's soul but in the state kettle. Abstruse, toothless hags augur Macbeth's fate. Macbeth is a sloven killer. He lacks the mineraled innards of a conscienceless Iago, the perfect metaphysical brigand, whose sleep is as a babe's soft-gummed dream—true heir of the State. Macbeth is weak, and the very nature that is weak in him, and should not exist at all, is the stumbling-block to a king's destiny. Lady Macbeth comes much closer to the ideal of first principles of slaughter. Her veins are swollen with the "race properties of the nation." Gore does not trammel her purpose:

> . . . make thick my blood:
> Store up the access and passage to remorse,
> That no compunctious visitings of nature
> Shake my fell purpose . . .
> And take my milk for all, you murdering ministers.

But Lady Macbeth also fails when she becomes insane, and this is her one "unhistorical" act. Her murders make her equal to History's role, but the puling sickness of her brain is mere literature and personal diary. This is a human lapse and not the stuff for the World's stage. It is an axiom in Shakespearian drama that Nature, Man and King can never coexist. Upon this postulate rests the divine right of kings.

The flaw in Macbeth is his mortality. Is not uncrowned Richard common sod, and does he not know it, and do not his utterances fall away when there is no crown to solemnize them? Can anyone mistake these bald and *undressed* lines:

> RICHARD: For you have but mistook me all this while:
> I live with bread like you, feel want,
> Taste grief, need friends: subjected thus,
> How can you say to me, I am king?

Or listen to Bolingbroke, the unsteady, profane and potential usurper, expressing a commoner's gratitude to his peers: "Evermore, thanks, the exchequer of the poor . . ."

Macbeth lacks the prophetic state vision. He is a *common* soldier without Neronian, sybaritic vices and without the apocalyptic leakages of the magian, Hitler. The mystical sorcerer of the modern state is himself healed and purified by the blood-purge. Otherwise, like Lady Macbeth, he would go mad. However, the necromantic slaughterer never needs the mortal relief and ease of the madhouse. Unlike Lady Macbeth, Hitler need never unsex his nature, mire upon and gall his natural human milk, to act out his role: for his bloody deeds will engender no stalking bloodless visions. He elevates execution into a mystical satyriasis of the fatherland: he hires no mean highwaymen to perform his offices, but organizes a Dionysiac espionage of fanatical novitiates. In a totalitarian country, the once despised informer becomes a state bacchant who is assisted by the people in his flesh-tearing rites. The public is the choric fury and the nemesis of the nation!

3. THE STATE KETTLE

Hitler, like the ancient priestess in Achaia, drinks, as Sir James Frazer writes, "the fresh blood of a bull before (he) descended into the cave to prophesy." The proletariat today is the body of sacrifice which gives rebirth to the fatherland just as the Mithraic bull, identified with the people, was burnt and eaten by them so that total oneness and resurrection could be symbolized. In countries with dictatorships these rites are closely guarded: the Greek-Catholic Church of Russia must necessarily be disestablished: the war against the German Protestant ecclesiastics is more profoundly *demonic*. The state makes its own images, saints, icons, blows its own winds and incantations and drinks its own Cabalistical broth out of the State Kettle. New and devoted gods are as important as faithful armies. Jesus must be cast aside as a useless and broken relic when the War and Lust deities, Thor and Wotan, can serve better.

The populace exchanges one set of pieties for another, but the beliefs and the fetishes are essentially the same: crosses, icons, madonnas give way to effigies of Stalin and Hitler. The need of a secular mariolatry for a more "scientific" citizen must be gratified. Screen stars are more immediate and practical as purification and expressive devices than the worship of remote constellations. The distinction between Zeus, Jupiter, Osiris and Popeye the Sailor, the comics and the goddesses of the screen is not in science but in poetics.

The cave rites of the state today are performed in the rotting apocalyptic darkness of the movie-grotto: the American goes into this hidden pit where his nerves are appeased by mechanical motion-picture deities. He takes his revenge upon the fates, misery, unemployment, sexual starvation, through the sadic furies of Popeye the Sailor: the little mechanized underdog demolishes walls, furniture, hurtles pianos, chairs, dishes, and makes the whole world propertyless. Comics, automobile accidents, tabloid sex crimes take the place of sacrifice. The Little American *breaks out* into laughter over the tombstone cartoons of Walt Disney. American Humor is as insidious as kneeling and prayer.

The megalopolitan plebs require brand-new taboos and images; so the Mary-cult is supplanted by the leader-cult, Christianity is superseded by Marx, and shamanism by communism.

Maximus aroused the contempt of the Roman Plebs because he had once kept sheep in Thrace, and this made him an easy and popular victim of his rival. However, the pastoral shepherd and swineherd have come into their own; a new set of occupation-fetishes has made it possible for a house painter and a Georgian peasant to symbolize the national superstitious mysticism of an industrial proletariat. The brown shirt and the red army uniform are substituted for the state and the crown; and the mesmerized vassal stalks across the stage of World History like his master! There is a subtle hoax in this act that a simple, obedient proletarian, mummer can never know.

The "awakened" worker is the soviet Osirian corn-maker and god of May Day, crops, socialized cattle and agriculture, who himself *requires* a leader, a communist shaman who has sole power over the mystical collective hands, eyes and genital organs of the Workers' Fatherland. The mystical identity between state and the proletariat always makes the latter the sacrificial flesh and blood of the former.

The soviet worker plants, reaps, mines and manufactures for the next generation. His own life and limbs are dismembered and put into the earth, into the Fatherland, like Osiris, so that he can *seed* the future. The blood sacrifice and ritual are merely repeated; the proletarian godhead, the masses, must forever devour itself to fertilize soviet soil. The image, the benign Buddha-Marxian manikin, the Byzantine icon, Stalin, standing on the Kremlin walls, is immune: it is always the worker's body made of corn, flesh and bone, that is buried in the ground.

Each generation must deeply drink its own tragic life.

It is a perverted generation that feeds upon its own vitals and limbs. Ivan Karamazov's denunciation of self-laceration is muffled in the roar of accelerated five-year plans, the demonic mechanization of the city: "Surely I haven't suffered, simply that I, my crimes and my sufferings, may manure the soil of the future harmony for somebody else. I want to see with my own eyes the hind lie down with the lion and the victim rise up and embrace his murderer." What perils will ensue when the Russians learn that all they have labored for is to be given away to cozening Immortality, to oblivion, aye, even to their own children.

A whole people can be taught to swaddle its tenderest expectancies in its own cerements and to yearn for its dissolution in the mistaken belief that its sacrifice will heal and ennoble men who have not yet been born. National self-immolation is so rooted in state-morality that men and women die more loftily for the race than they live for it. Suicide squads are the undeniable signs of the death-cult that is abroad today and not the tokens of a deep moral fervor. Dying then becomes man's lucent and soul-flaked star!

The dictator, the communist man-god, Stalin, heals the collective consciousness, regulates marriage, abortions, divorces, decrees new customs, mores, larger families; he controls rest, labor, worship, art and science, letters, ceremonies, parades, fetes and hates. His picture hangs in all public places and in private homes, and is a complete substitute for the saint and the relic. André Gide writes: "I did not enter a single inhabited room, even the humblest and most sordid, without remarking a portrait of Stalin hanging on the wall, in the same place no doubt where the icon used to be."

The leader has his own Marxian magicians who exorcise

dissenters, "wreckers," saboteurs and fetish-breakers of the soviet Delphic oracles. He who criticizes eats his own totem—the leader, the cult, the doctrine and the state. These public wizards in turn become the enemies within and are banished or executed when crops fall off, industry lags and general discontent prevails.

The Marxian logic of exorcism and taboo is a national surrogate for ancient blood rites. The public hate-festivals which all dictators hold are based on homeopathic magic: books and effigies are burnt in the same spirit as images of fat and grain, made to resemble an enemy, were buried by primitive people. National memorial hymns are used to arouse cult-like superstitions about other peoples. Class hatred is a substitute for human sacrifice: the masses, through state victory chants, book burning, giant war parades of tanks, airplane maneuvers, robotized phalanxes of soldiers, devour their enemies.

The proletariat, the effigies of Lenin and Stalin, the priestly "party line," have taken the place of the bull, the monstrance and Holy Writ. The mummy of Lenin rests in the sacred Kremlin: the embalmed corpse lies there as saint and venerabilia for the masses to gaze upon as "the grave of Zeus, the great God of Greece, was shown to visitors in Crete." Mummification is scarcely a "scientific Marxian" practice of an emancipated people.

Poor humanity, forever rending its own limbs and drinking its own blood so that it can resurrect itself. Like a pharaoh, man lies in his tomb with a pancake and corn-meal god at his side and so embalms his heart and brain, not knowing that they alone can rise from the grave and make him immortal! O, when will he throw away idols: the states, the toy tanks, war games and flags, the fatherland? Moses took us out of the primitive age of Baal and

the golden calf, when he destroyed all the graven images.

Man will roll the Sisyphean rock until he demolishes the superstition of the state and the leader. There is the legend that Empedocles threw himself into the crater of Mt. Etna so that no one would ever know that he had died; but the story, told by the men who lived after him, is that the crater belched forth his sandals! It is a beautiful story and a joy-giving irony, and the heart that can contain such mirthful sanities can laugh and weep. O, let man laugh the *gods* out of this world so that the heart can live in it!

SELECTED ANN ARBOR PAPERBACKS
works of enduring mer

AA 1 **THE WRITER AND HIS CRAFT** Roy W. Cowden, ed.

AA 2 **ELIZABETHAN PLAYS AND PLAYERS** G. B. Harrison

AA 3 **THE INTELLECTUAL MILIEU OF JOHN DRYDEN** Louis I. Bredvold

AA 6 **RICHARD CRASHAW** Austin Warren

AA 11 **LITERATURE AND PSYCHOLOGY** F. L. Lucas

AA 12 **THIS WAS A POET: EMILY DICKINSON** George Frisbie Whicher

AA 16 **SHAKESPEARE AT WORK, 1592-1603** G. B. Harrison

AA 26 **RONSARD: PRINCE OF POETS** Morris Bishop

AA 32 **THE SONG OF ROLAND** Translated by C. K. Scott Moncrieff

AA 33 **RAGE FOR ORDER** Austin Warren

AA 36 **NEW BEARINGS IN ENGLISH POETRY** F. R. Leavis

AA 40 **THE SUBLIME** Samuel H. Monk

AA 43 **LITERATURE AND REVOLUTION** Leon Trotsky

AA 46 **THE ART OF LITERATURE** Arthur Schopenhauer

AA 58 **SEBASTOPOL** Leo Tolstoi

AA 63 **POEMS FROM THE GREEK ANTHOLOGY** Translated by Kenneth Rexroth

AA 64 **THE SATYRICON—PETRONIUS** Translated by William Arrowsmith

AA 68 **AUBREY'S BRIEF LIVES** John Aubrey

AA 70 **SCENES FROM THE BATHHOUSE And Other Stories of Communist Russia** M. Zoshchenk

AA 81 **THE LOYALTIES OF ROBINSON JEFFERS** Radcliffe Squires

AA 82 **MILTON'S KNOWLEDGE OF MUSIC** Sigmund Spaeth

AA 85 **THE COMPLETE POETRY** Catullus

AA 87 **THE CLOUD MESSENGER** Kalidasa

AA 89 **THE INTERIOR DISTANCE** Georges Poulet

AA 91 **THE BOW AND THE LYRE: The Art of Robert Browning** Roma A. King, Jr.

AA 101 **CONTEMPORARY FRENCH POETRY** Alexander Aspel and Donald Justice, ed.

AA 102 **TO THE YOUNG WRITER** A. L. Bader, ed.

AA 113 **CHEKHOV AND OTHER ESSAYS** Leon Shestov

AA 116 **GREEK ORATIONS** W. Robert Connor, ed.

AA 117 **THE STORY OF THE ILIAD** E. T. Owen

AA 125 **THE STRUCTURE OF COMPLEX WORDS** William Empson

AA 128 **CAN THESE BONES LIVE** Edward Dahlberg

AA 132 **PARADISE LOST AND THE SEVENTEENTH CENTURY READER** B. Rajan

For a complete list of Ann Arbor Paperback titles write:
THE UNIVERSITY OF MICHIGAN PRESS / ANN ARBOR